Faith

JOEL SIEGEL

Simple Faith
©2017 Siegel Ministries, Inc.

The New Testament in Modern Speech (Weymouth New Testament)
Public Domain

Contents

. . . . Nevertheless, when the Son of Man comes, will he find faith on earth?

Luke 18:8b

Preface – introduction

I was sitting on the edge of my bed one evening, about to lay down, when God spoke to me. His voice was not audible in the natural realm, but was nevertheless strong and authoritative. This voice, reverberating on the inside of me with a commanding tone of proclamation, spoke two words: *FAITH COMES*. Although these two words were not entirely unfamiliar to me, I was still startled at the suddenness of this visitation.

I somehow knew there was more that the Spirit wanted to say, so I quickly reached for something to write with. I had the sense that this phrase was part of a sermon outline, with more points to follow, and I was correct. As soon as I was ready to write, three more phrases – more points to the sermon – were spoken. These last three phrases were spoken in slightly softer tones than the first. Here are all four phrases that the Lord spoke to me that night:

1. Faith Comes
2. Faith Says
3. Faith Moves
4. Faith Wins

My spiritual father, Rev. Kenneth E. Hagin, used to say that when God gives you a sermon, you can preach it over and over. He would then add, somewhat jokingly, that when you work up a sermon by yourself, it can hardly stand one preaching. This sermon – woven throughout this book – is based on the outline above, given to me by the Spirit of God. I have preached it many times, and intend to do so for the rest of my life, for the principles contained in these four short phrases have changed my life.

Chapter 1
God's Part, Our Part

The Bible is a big book, filled with great stories from centuries past, but really, all the stories are one story. The Bible is the story of redemption: man's deliverance from sin and the effects of sin. From Adam's fall to Messiah's death and resurrection, from Israel's deliverance through the Red Sea to the renovation of the earth, the pages of Scripture echo one great theme: *We have been delivered. We are redeemed.* The reason we have the holy scriptures is to understand how God accomplished our redemption; how He got us out of the mess we got ourselves into.

But why so many stories? Why all the letters and accounts? Because, redemption is not something that works all by itself. It's not automatic. There are components, all of which must work together if redemption is to work as it should. The Bible is our instruction manual, teaching us how God's great plan of redemption works. It shows us how to take our place, do our part, and possess what is ours.

The Bible is big because God is big. That doesn't mean, however, that the things of God are complicated. On the contrary, they are not. The components necessary to access and enjoy the benefits of redemption are few and they are simple, repeated throughout Scripture for clarity and emphasis. (Even with all that repetition, many still fail to recognize and cooperate with God's principles.) The components that make redemption work can be divided into two categories: God's part and man's part.

There's a God-side and a man-side to every spiritual transaction, yet many remain ignorant of this fact. Religious leaders persistently herald the lie that there's nothing we can do about the circumstances in our life but leave them in God's all-knowing care. Well-meaning (but uninformed) people tell us that we can never really know how things will turn out, or how (or even if) God will act. Such beliefs are dangerous, leading many dedicated, God-loving people into defeat. We must renew our minds to God's truth, allowing His Word to form (and, if necessary, reshape) our beliefs. We must become established in the fact that almost everything God does requires man's participation.

We said that redemption is all about man's deliverance from sin and the effects of sin. Just what are those effects? Anything that works death, decay, or destruction. Anything that robs the believer from experiencing an abundant quality of life. Two areas in particular, sickness and poverty, came into the earth along with sin and are part of the curse from which we have been redeemed. Because of Jesus, we can escape the bondage of sin, sickness, and poverty, and instead enjoy righteousness, health, and a full supply.

GOD'S PART

God's part in redemption was to provide all that we need for an eternal relationship with Him, and all that we need for success and victory here in this life. Nowhere is this amazing provision seen more clearly than in one of Scripture's most beloved verses:

> *For God so loved the world, that he gave his only Son,*
> *that whoever believes in him should not perish but have*
> *eternal life.*

> *John 3:16*

God loved. God gave. God's giving is the action of His love. (It would be accurate to say that giving is the highest expression of love.) Because God loved us, He gave us all we need. He loved so we could *have*. Although His love made eternal life available, we see in this verse that His part is not the only part required. Man has a part as well. The last part of this verse shows that he who believes is the one who receives, or possesses, eternal life. God's part and man's part work together so that man can have what God gives.

The *giving* of God (His part) has another name in the Bible: *grace*. God's grace is every bit as amazing as the famous hymn states and is a major theme throughout the New Testament.

Grace is the flow of God's love in you, to you, and through you, bringing His ability and blessings to your life. When you think of the grace of God, think of the giving of God. Grace gives.

> For if, because of one man's trespass, death reigned through that one man, much more will **those who receive the abundance of grace** and the free gift of righteousness reign in life through the one man Jesus Christ.
>
> Romans 5:17

God has made abundant provision for our lives by His grace, but notice that His grace must be *received*. When we say that *grace gives*, we mean exactly that, yet God's giving doesn't make His provision a reality in our lives. Giving is just one part – one side – of the equation. What God gives must also be received. Only when God's giving is received do His blessings become a reality in our lives.

OUR PART

Someone can buy you a gift and ship it to your house, but their giving doesn't place the item inside your house. You must receive the gift by opening your door, picking up the package, and bringing it inside. You didn't pay for it or send it, but you did have to accept it. You had to *receive*, or *take*, what was given. That's the way it is with the things of God. Everything God gives must be received. If we want His gifts to become a reality in our lives, we must discover what's been given and take those things into our lives. We must receive.

Religion doesn't recognize the receiving side of our redemption. Religious-minded Christians choose to believe that God will do it all; that His blessings will just fall upon us, magically appearing in our lives. The religious person's beliefs are more aligned with superstition and fantasy than with the principles of Biblical Christianity. Yes, God has a part to do. In fact, His part is by far the hardest part. He paid the price to make redemption's benefits eternally available. He has done everything except our part, for He cannot force His blessings into our lives. We must do our part. We must receive.

> For **by grace** you have been saved **through faith**. And
> this is not your own doing; it is the gift of God, not a
> result of works, so that no one may boast.
>
> *Ephesians 2:8-9*

God's part – giving – is called *grace*. Our part – receiving – is called *faith*. Faith is how the believer receives all that God has given. It's the act of picking up the blessings He has delivered to us and taking them into our life. Our salvation, indeed, all the blessings of God, are given by His grace and received by our faith. Grace gives. Faith receives.

Redemption's benefits are ours for the taking. In many respects, God's part is done. He has stocked the shelves of our lives, so to speak, with His many blessings. Now it's up to us; it's time for our part. We must, by faith, receive all that He's given. God's great blessings are sitting at the doorstep of your life, waiting for faith to reach out and bring them inside. Your job, for the rest of your life, is to become skillful at receiving what God has given. Your job is to learn faith.

Chapter 2
Contenders

*Beloved, although I was very eager to write to you about our common salvation, I found it necessary to write appealing to you to **contend for the faith** that was once for all delivered to the saints.*

Jude 1:3

Jude's lone chapter in the Bible contains some of the most forceful, no-punches-pulled language in Scripture. He speaks, not casually, but with urgency, exhorting the Body of Christ to listen up and get things in gear. He begins his letter with a passionate plea about one particular subject: the subject of faith.

Here, we see the author speaking of *the faith*. (We often use this phrase *the faith* to speak of Christianity in a general sense. Many have heard someone talk about another person, saying, *They have come to the faith*. All of us have heard the phrase *Keep the faith*). We use this phrase *the faith* to paint Christianity with a broad brush, as it were, but that's not how the phrase is used in this passage.

The word *the* is not even present in the original Greek language. (This is true, not just of this passage, but in many of the passages where the phrase *the faith* is found.) It should not read *the faith*, but simply *faith*. Let's discover what Jude was really saying here:

> *Contend for faith, as it was originally delivered to the saints.*

Jude was speaking, not about Christianity in general, but specifically about the subject of faith: the believer's part in receiving from God.

Jude was saying, in essence, *Guys, I wanted to write to you in a more general fashion about our common beliefs, but I was arrested on the inside, compelled to write to you specifically about faith as you originally learned it.* For Jude to have sensed such an urgency, there must have been something askew [crooked] in the Body. For him to specify faith's *original* teaching (*once for all*), there must have come a replacement teaching: a false version of faith masquerading as the real thing. Indeed, there was. Jude, in the next verse, gives us a peek into the circumstances which threatened to wipe out the purity of the believers' faith.

> *For certain people have crept in unnoticed who long ago were designated for this condemnation, ungodly people,*

who pervert the grace of our God *into sensuality and deny our only Master and Lord, Jesus Christ.*

Jude 1:4

BAD GRACE

When referencing the believer's tainted faith, Jude understood the cause to be people who crept in with wrong teaching and twisted beliefs. These people didn't focus their teaching on the subject of faith, however, but on the subject of grace. Jude told the believers to contend for faith because certain individuals had come in and *perverted the grace of God.*

At first glance, this doesn't make much sense. Why didn't Jude tell the Church to contend for *grace* as it was once delivered to the saints? Why did he talk so urgently about faith in one verse and then point to errors surrounding grace in the next? Because grace and faith are connected. Wrong thinking about grace will lead to wrong thinking about faith.

Remember, grace is God's part in redemption. Faith is our part. Our part is a response to His part (receiving what He has given). If we fail to correctly view God's part, we will misunderstand our part. For someone to pervert, or twist, the grace of God means that they believe incorrectly about God's love and giving (the essence of grace). Regrettably, many do believe wrong about these things. The Bible warns of two major errors where the subject of God's grace is concerned.

WORKS

The first error is the belief that for us to receive God's blessings, we must incessantly work to try and qualify. Simply put, people believe that we must *earn* the blessings of redemption. Even if they have been taught otherwise, condemnation, guilt, and a lack of understanding of the Word causes them to feel unworthy. They feel as though they must always work harder to try to gain God's approval. In their minds, God will only move on their behalf if they act good enough.

We hear much teaching about what *we must do* for God to be able to bless us. There's certainly a truth there (I teach these things myself), but if such teaching isn't presented in a balanced fashion, Christians will develop a works-mentality whereby they try to earn the favor of God. Paul addressed this grace-perversion often throughout his writings, in verses such as this one that we saw earlier:

> For by grace you have been saved through faith. And this
> is not your own doing; **it is the gift of God, not a result**
> **of works,** so that no one may boast.
>
> *Ephesians 2:8-9*

How does this error affect our faith? If a person thinks he or she must earn the blessings of God, they will always be working but never receiving. Always trying, but never obtaining. They will end up frustrated with the things of God, because they are forever *doing* without being able to lay hold of the object of their faith. The things of God always seem just beyond their grasp. In their mind, the things they need from God are all up to them, and their performance always seems to fall short.

This error of working for our blessings is the ditch on one side of the road where grace is concerned. There is also a ditch on the other side of the road that is just as devious and dangerous. It's this second ditch to which Jude was referring.

NO WORKS

The first error concerning grace is the belief that receiving from God is all up to us. The second error – the ditch on the other side of the road – is the belief that everything is up to God: that we have no part to play in receiving (no work to do). With each new generation, these two errors manage to circulate throughout the Body of Christ.

If we believe that grace means God does everything and we do nothing – that everything that we receive is by *grace alone* – then the door is thrust open to an even greater error. If what we do doesn't affect our receiving, then why does it matter what we do at all? If everything is up to God, restraint can be cast aside and we can live to please our own fleshly desires. The frustration of the first error – the works mentality – often leads people to swing over to the looseness of the second error. The truth, as always, is in the middle of the road. We must seek the place of soundness and balance.

Grace *does* mean that God has done it all, in a sense. Providing our redemption was all God (our human efforts contributing nothing to redemption's price). Yet, without us doing our part, redemption's benefits go unrealized. Our part is to receive what God has given: not working for it, not earning it, but simply receiving through faith. We must understand that, although we don't work to earn our blessings, there is effort required in order to believe. There is such a thing as the *work of faith*.

> Then they said to him, "What must we do, to be doing the works of God?" Jesus answered them, "**This is the work of God, that you believe** in him whom he has sent."
>
> *John 6:28-29*

The believer must be engaged in the work of believing. Believing is the work of faith: our responsibility in receiving from God. Jude exhorted the New Testament believers to *contend* for the faith. Contending is something that occurs with great purpose and effort. It's the opposite of relaxing, where one sits around doing nothing. We've all heard of *heavyweight contenders*: those who square off in the boxing ring, trained and poised to deliver the knockout blow. Contending, unlike relaxing, is work.

Understanding that God did everything in providing our redemption is a proper view of grace. Understanding that redemption's benefits cannot enter our lives without our participation is a proper view of faith. Everything we receive from God is by His grace, through our faith.

12

ONCE FOR ALL

Jude was the younger brother of the Lord Jesus. When he spoke of *the faith that was once for all delivered to the saints*, he was no doubt referring primarily to that which his brother, Jesus, had taught. Having watched his own brother suffer and die, it's easy to understand why he would passionately protect His ministry. The fact that others were attempting to modify His message was irksome to Jude. What Christ delivered was *once for all*: unchangeable and eternal.

So what did Jesus teach about faith? Only one thing. (People are sometimes shocked when I say that, yet it's true. Although He often made statements like, *Where's your faith?* or, *I have not found such great faith*, those were comments, not a teaching.) The essence of Jesus' teaching on faith was, *If you'll get it and use it, you can receive anything you need from God.* Jesus taught about a faith that receives. Not just a faith that passively *agrees*, but a faith that aggressively acts. This kind of faith is what Jesus delivered to us. This is what Jude saw slipping away. This is what we must contend for.

> *Jesus answered and said unto them, Verily I say unto you, If ye have faith, and doubt not, ye shall not only do this which is done to the fig tree, but also if ye shall say unto this mountain, Be thou removed, and be thou cast into the sea; it shall be done. And all things, whatsoever ye shall ask in prayer, believing, ye shall receive.*
>
> *Matthew 21:21-22 (KJV)*

We can only contend for faith if we understand it. We can only operate in faith if we can identify it: recognizing how it looks, sounds, and acts. Many people try to use faith without understanding the principles of faith. Such people invariably operate a false version of faith. They are faith *pretenders* instead of faith *contenders*. Let's learn faith, obtain faith, operate faith, and enjoy the results. The chapters that follow will equip you to successfully use your faith.

Chapter 3

The Place of Faith

The scriptures are clear that faith is all about receiving from God. Jesus taught about it. Jude fought for it. People have actually died for it. It's no surprise, then, that the devil passionately opposes the message of faith. He hates it; it's his kryptonite. This amazing statement by the Apostle Paul illustrates just how great a threat faith is to the devil's kingdom:

> *In all circumstances take up the shield of faith, with which you can extinguish all the flaming darts of the evil one.*
>
> *Ephesians 6:16*

Our faith is the devil's defeat, neutralizing every one of his attacks. No wonder he dislikes it so. Put yourself, just for a moment, in the devil's shoes. You spend years working to place a person's life in an irreversible state of bondage. Then, one act of faith undoes all that work. How frustrating it must be to be Satan. We can easily see why the devil would go to extreme lengths to pervert and oppose faith. His desire to taint the subject is strategic and ongoing. What's surprising, however, is that the greatest opposition to faith comes from within the Body of Christ.

unclear

The message of faith is so obscured and misunderstood that, if you randomly approached ten Christians on the street and asked them if they were using their faith to receive anything from God, six or seven would have no idea at all what you were talking about. The other three or four might reply, *Oh, you must be talking about that name it and claim it stuff.* Sadly, many in the Body are opposed to the message of faith.

Unknowledgeable believers everywhere consider the faith message to be a joke, a destructive heresy that resembles the far-out doctrines of a cult more than the time-honored truths of God's Word (hence, the mocking nickname *Name it and claim it*). Religious leaders have promoted this distaste for faith, their denominational beliefs clouding the clear teachings of Scripture. We must have more respect for the written Word of God than for traditional religious views.

Although many passionately oppose the message of faith, many others hold a less negative view. While they aren't necessarily opposed to the message, they don't fully embrace it. They think that people such as myself hold an extreme view, overemphasizing the subject. They're okay with the idea of faith as long as it's general and vague: no more than a side issue with nothing

16

required of them. I'm sorry, but that's not what Jesus died for, nor is it what Jude told us to contend for.

It's true that *any* subject, faith included, can be pushed to the extreme, resulting in error. What, then, is the proper balance? How much is too much? There's only one place to find out: the Word of God. The following scriptures help define the place of faith in the believer's life.

> *For by grace you have been* **saved through faith.** *And this is not your own doing; it is the gift of God.*
>
> *Ephesians 2:8*

This is the third time that we have looked at this verse. It's significant, for it shows how one receives from God. Everything that we receive from God – salvation, healing, deliverance, blessing, provision, etc. – comes to us the same way. All the blessings of God are given by His grace and are received through our faith. This verse speaks of being *saved*, a term which refers to the born-again experience. A person cannot be born again without faith. How important is faith? You can't be saved without it. You can't receive from God without it. Sounds important to me.

> *And without faith it is impossible to please him, for whoever would draw near to God must believe that he exists and that he rewards those who seek him.*
>
> *Hebrews 11:6*

In answering the question, *Is faith important?* one must ask, *Is pleasing God important?* Every believer would agree that it is. There's only one way to please God, however. Faith. If we desire to please God every day, we should be interested in using our faith every day. Faith is so much more than the occasional *extra push* that we add to our prayers when we really want something. Faith is part of our everyday life, just as pleasing God should be an everyday occurrence. You can't please God without faith.

Here's another verse that shows the importance of faith:

> *For everyone who has been born of God overcomes the world. And this is the victory that has overcome the world—our faith.*
>
> *1 John 5:4*

Our faith – not the faith of our pastor, prayer partner, spouse, or friends – is the victory that overcomes the world. What does this verse mean when it speaks of overcoming the world? It's speaking of anything in the world that might come against us. Any test, trial, or opposition. If what you're dealing with is in the world (and what difficulty isn't?), it can be overcome through faith. How amazing! Our faith – or to put it more personally, *your faith* – can overcome any difficulty that comes against you. Your faith is your victory.

How important is faith? It's the difference between victory and defeat. Our victory isn't decided by God. He lays victory or defeat before us.

Here's another verse (actually four verses) illustrating the place of faith:

> *Behold, his soul is puffed up; it is not upright within him, but **the righteous shall live by his faith.***
>
> *Habakkuk 2:4*

> *For I am not ashamed of the gospel, for it is the power of God for salvation to everyone who believes, to the Jew first and also to the Greek. For in it the righteousness of God is revealed from faith for faith, as it is written, "**The righteous shall live by faith.**"*
>
> *Romans 1:16-17*

> *Now it is evident that no one is justified before God by the law, for "**The righteous shall live by faith.**"*
>
> *Galatians 3:11*

> *"But **my righteous one shall live by faith**, and if he shrinks back, my soul has no pleasure in him."*
>
> *Hebrews 10:38*

No less than four times in the Word of God we are told that *the righteous shall live by faith.* This all-encompassing phrase shows that faith is to have a place in our lives equal to the food that we eat or the air that we breathe. How important is faith? It's our life. We can't live as we should without it. We can't please God without it. We can't be saved without it. Our victory in the world depends on it. Faith isn't just important, it's everything.

Notice one more of these great verses:

For we walk by faith, not by sight.

2 Corinthians 5:7

We walk (ordering our life and making our decisions) by what we believe rather than what we see, hear, or feel. We put the truth of God's Word above what our physical senses understand to be true. Stop and think about this for a moment. Does God really expect us to discount natural evidence, walking away from what we see and feel, in order to follow Him? He sure does, and it's one of the greatest privileges of the Christian life.

How much faith is too much? There's no such thing. God will never tell you to back off and believe Him less. He'll never ask you to balance out your faith with unbelief. Faith is His delight. Finding it in us thrills Him. Critics can criticize all they want. They can live in defeat while I enjoy victory. I choose victory. I choose faith. I am convinced that, in the believer's life, there's nothing more important than faith.

Chapter 4
Faith Comes

On that night when God spoke to me, He said four things. The first thing He said was also the loudest thing. I believe He spoke in strong tones so as to give this first phrase a special emphasis. The next several chapters reflect that emphasis. The first phrase that the Spirit spoke to me that night was, *Faith comes*. That phrase is a direct quote from Scripture.

> So **faith comes** from hearing, and hearing through the
> word of Christ.
>
> *Romans 10:17*

Since faith *comes*, we know that it isn't a static commodity; in other words, it may be present at different levels at different times in the believer's life. Just because a person is born again doesn't mean he or she possesses the faith that's needed for the circumstances they might encounter. For a person to have faith,

faith must come. Then, in order to maintain faith, faith must continue to come. The *coming* of faith is the believer's responsibility.

While the born-again person doesn't enter the Christian life possessing a fully developed faith, he or she does have the capacity for faith. The believer is a *new creation* (2 Corinthians 5:17): a new person with the ability to believe and receive from God. We must take the faith He gives us at the new birth – our *starter portion* of faith, as it were – and develop it.

HEARING

Since it's our job to ensure that faith comes, we must have a solid understanding of how it comes. The verse above tells us clearly and simply: *faith comes from hearing*. Hearing – not straining, trying, wishing, hoping, praying, crying, begging, or worrying – is how faith comes.

Some may have been told (perhaps by a friend or their pastor) that they need to bring faith to their situation. With tones of desperation, that person might reply, *I know. I'm trying to believe.* Although they mean well, they must understand that it's not trying that brings faith, it's hearing. We don't *try* to believe, we *hear* to believe. For faith to come, the believer must hear.

Although faith comes by hearing, many nevertheless pursue other paths to faith. Some try to substitute praying for hearing. They pray, *O Lord, strengthen my faith.* How exactly is He supposed to do that? Recite a magical incantation? Speak a word of command: *My child, be strengthened in faith?* No, that's not how faith comes. Praying for faith, no matter how heartfelt, does not release the believer from his or her responsibility of hearing. The only way God can answer such a prayer is by bringing the believer the opportunity to hear. Faith comes by hearing.

What, then, must we hear? If we want faith in God, we must hear from God.

When opposing circumstances challenge your faith, many voices will compete for your attention. Well-meaning people, the devil, and even the circumstances themselves will want to help direct your life. We must shut out these other voices, instead hearing from God. We don't just need to hear *about* Him, we need to hear *from* Him. How does one hear from God? The main way a person hears from God is by hearing the Word of God. Notice again our text:

> *So faith comes from hearing, and **hearing through the word of Christ**.*
>
> *Romans 10:17*

Hearing God's Word is how faith in God comes.

VITAMINS

People place their faith in many different things. Some, for example, have faith in vitamins. They continually talk about supplements and vitamins and how religious they are about their daily regimen. How did they come to develop such strong faith in vitamins? They heard about vitamins. Then, they heard some more. They continued to hear about vitamins until they were convinced that vitamins were their answer. Faith in vitamins comes from hearing about vitamins.

What we hear is important, yet *who* we hear from is also important. If a person is trying to sell vitamins, it's important not just that they know about vitamins, but also that they have a strong level of personal credibility. If the vitamin salesman is known to be a swindler or charlatan, it's doubtful that people will believe much of what he or she says. Your faith in vitamins is based not just on what someone is telling you, but also on who that person is. Your faith is in a person as well as a product.

For a person to have faith in God, he or she must believe His Word. In order to believe His Word, the person must have some idea of the credibility – the character and ability – of the author of those words. Thank God, we know much about His character and ability. It's easy to measure God's ability: He spoke and the world was created. All power, wisdom, and knowledge are His. There's never an issue with God's ability. Or His character.

We spoke in the first chapter about how big the Bible is and how thoroughly it speaks to the different areas of our life. Another reason for the bigness of the Bible? It shows the consistency of God's character. We have not just weeks, but millennia worth of history of how God acts. Of the many important things we learn about God, one of the most precious is this: *If He says it, He'll do it.* His Word is absolutely reliable; His character, impeccable; His truth, unchangeable; His power, unstoppable. He is, in every way, infallible.

God is not man, that he should lie, or a son of man, that he should change his mind. Has he said, and will he not do it? Or has he spoken, and will he not fulfill it?

Numbers 23:19

The One who called you is completely dependable. If he said it, he'll do it!

1 Thessalonians 5:24 (MSG)

God has never lied to anyone. He's never promised and then failed to deliver. He is completely trustworthy, one hundred percent dependable. He's never let anyone down. His love for us is unwavering, His faithfulness unbroken. He's not about to ruin His perfect track record by failing us in our time of need. We must become settled in the fact that the One in whom we place our trust is worthy of that trust. His character is worthy of our full faith.

We can confidently rest in God's character and ability, fully trusting in who He is. That, however, is not enough for faith. We must also discover what He's said. Both kinds of knowledge – the knowledge of who He is and the knowledge of what He's said – are necessary for faith.

WHAT DID I TELL YOU?

If you got to know me, I'm sure you would like me. I'm not perfect, but I have enough of God in my life that, if you like Him, you'd like me. I'm a person of my word. I endeavor to be faithful to my promises. I have a pretty good track record when it comes to my character.

If you came to me and said, *Joel, I'm believing that you will give me a thousand dollars*, it would be apparent to me that you really weren't in faith. You may *think* you're believing that (and indeed may have convinced yourself of that) but you would just be a faith pretender, not a faith contender. If I asked you, *Why are you believing that I'll give you a thousand dollars?* you might answer, *Because I've gotten to know you and I think you're a really great guy.* You're right. I am a really great guy, but that's not enough knowledge for faith.

Knowing that I'm a great guy is important, for it brings knowledge of my character. It tells you who I am and gives you confidence that my word is reliable. Knowledge of my character is important, but it's only one part of the knowledge necessary for faith.

I might have entered a room where you were and mentioned that I had a thousand dollars in my pocket. You may have become encouraged, realizing that I'm both a great guy and a blessed guy. You discovered that I had the ability to give you a thousand dollars. Knowledge of my ability (like knowledge of my character) is important, but that knowledge alone won't bring faith.

Besides knowing *who I am* (my character and ability), you need to know *what I've said.*

The only way you could really believe that I would give you a thousand dollars is if you knew I had a thousand dollars, knew that my word was reliable, *and* if I specifically told you that I was giving *you* that thousand dollars. I may have gone so far as to announce to the people in the room that I had a thousand dollars that I was giving away, but if I didn't specifically say that I was giving it to *you*, you would have no basis upon which to exercise faith for my money. You can't have faith for *my* thousand dollars if I didn't tell you I was giving you my thousand dollars.

Yes, but I need a thousand dollars. Faith doesn't come by needing, it comes by hearing. *I don't care. I'm still going to believe for you to give me your thousand dollars.* Not without faith you're not. You can convince yourself of anything you want, but you can't believe that I will act on your behalf unless faith comes. Faith for my money only comes if you hear from me. You can't hear what I didn't say. The only way to really believe that I will give you my thousand dollars is for me to tell you that I am giving it to you.

Although this illustration of trying to believe for my money may seem silly, many people similarly decide to believe for things that God never promised. They convince themselves that God will bring to pass the things they have imagined, yet they never really heard from Him. They are deceived: destined for disappointment. If God said it, you can have faith for it. If God didn't say it, you can't have faith for it. We can only step out in faith when we have knowledge of who He is and what He's said.

Here are some interesting stories that illustrate the necessity of the two kinds of knowledge we have been speaking about:

I travelled with Rev. Kenneth E. Hagin for several years as

part of his crusade team. At one of our meetings, a lady came up and spoke to several of us on the team. She said that she was about to receive a large sum of money and would be giving each of us five thousand dollars. We were all young in ministry and life. Some had just started families and purchased homes. You can imagine how excited we got and how quickly we made plans for that money. To look at us, you would think that we were in faith, but that was not possible. We lacked part of the knowledge necessary for faith.

We had this lady's word – what she said – but really didn't know who she was. We lacked the knowledge of her character and ability. She may indeed have desired to bless us in the fashion she indicated, but did she actually possess those resources? And, if she did, would she be a person of her word, faithful to follow through? The answer, of course, was no. We never heard from her again.

Many years later, a gentleman I had never personally met promised a large sum of money to my ministry. When he did, I did not get excited, for I remembered the lady at Brother Hagin's crusade meeting. I had this man's word (just as I had that lady's word), but I had no knowledge of his character or ability.

I spoke with an acquaintance of mine – a minister whom I knew to be of strong integrity – who knew this man. He said to me, *Joel, this man has pledged similar sums to me before. Every single time, he has done exactly what he said he would do. He is honorable and exceedingly wealthy.* I now had enough knowledge to have faith in this man's promise. I had received, from a trusted source, knowledge of this man's character and ability. The knowledge of his *person* now accompanied my knowledge of his *promise*. He indeed followed through.

When it comes to believing God (we use the word *believe* interchangeably with the word *faith*. They mean the same thing and are often translated from the same Greek word), we need these two kinds of knowledge: knowledge of His character and ability, and knowledge of His promises. We need to know who He is as well as what He's said. The believer must become established in these two areas of truth.

Chapter 5

One Way

Receiving from God doesn't happen without faith. That means salvation, healing, deliverance, provision, etc. doesn't happen without faith. Faith does not work automatically, but works only as the believer remains involved and engaged, cooperating with the principles found in God's Word. We have responsibilities where our faith is concerned, including the responsibility to obtain faith. How is faith obtained? Only one way. Romans 10:17 tells us that *faith comes by hearing, and hearing through the Word of Christ.*

Hearing is the *only* way faith comes. It doesn't come through prayer. It can't be imparted through the laying on of hands. For faith to come, a person must hear. Many scriptures speak to this truth.

*In him you also, **when you heard** the word of truth, the gospel* *of your salvation, **and believed** in him, were sealed with the promised Holy Spirit.*

Ephesians 1:13

What happens before believing? Hearing. You can't believe the gospel without hearing the gospel.

*Let me ask you only this: Did you receive the Spirit by works of the law or by **hearing with faith**?*

Galatians 3:2

If a person received their answer by faith, we know that he or she first took time to hear.

What happens if a person doesn't hear? Faith doesn't come; it's not there. If it's not there, you can't use it. If you can't use it, you can't receive from God. If you can't receive from God, you'll have to go without your answer. God does not guarantee that we can receive our answer through any other means. Faith is it. If you want His help, you'll have to have faith.

The great English preacher, Smith Wigglesworth, made this statement:

There will come the day in the life of every person when he or she will need faith. If it's not there when they need it, that day will be a sad day.

I'm not interested in life's trials resulting in my defeat. I want to overcome; I want to win. If victory and success are in my control, I want to do my part to ensure that I succeed.

KINGDOM CURRENCY

Many years ago, there was a television commercial advertising VISA credit cards. That commercial spotlighted different travel destinations throughout the world, speaking of all the great things a person could do in those locations. Then they would say, *But bring your VISA, because they don't take American Express.* In those instances, VISA was the only accepted form of payment. If you didn't have a VISA card, you would be left out of the activity. Your lack of payment would make you a non-participant.

God has a good, rich quality of life planned for each of His children, yet each one must be able to conduct spiritual transactions in order to participate. You need the right currency. Just as VISA was the only accepted form of payment at those vacation destinations, faith is the only accepted form of payment in the Kingdom of God. If you have faith, you can accomplish much. If you lack faith, you can't conduct transactions in God's Kingdom. You are limited to the resources of this natural world.

If you need faith today (and you will, every day of your life), you'd better have some with you. Faith comes by hearing. If you haven't heard recently, faith isn't there.

I mentioned earlier that faith is not a static commodity, meaning it can be present at different levels at different times. That concept is very similar to how we use money. If you have money in your pocket and you spend it, what's in your pocket? Nothing. If you want to spend more money, what must you do? Steal? Counterfeit? No, you do what it takes to legally get more money. Money must come for you to be able to spend more money.

All of us have certain recurring expenses every month. If money isn't coming in for those expenses, there will soon be trouble. Why? Because money doesn't just come, it leaves. Every time you pay your electric bill or phone bill, money leaves. It must continue to come so that, the next time a bill is presented, sufficient funds are there. So it is with faith. When needs present themselves, they must be met with a robust supply of faith.

Faith doesn't just come, it also leaves. Like money, it leaves when you use it, and must be replaced. Unlike money, it doesn't just pile up if it goes unused.

Faith comes by hearing, but it leaves by not hearing. Many don't realize this. They think that because they have heard in the past, faith remains perpetually present, ready for use. Not so. Faith comes from *hearing*, not from *having heard*. There must be a continual hearing for faith to be continually present. The faith that came from previous hearings diminishes over time. We could say that faith has a relatively short shelf-life.

I pastored for eleven years in the Buffalo, New York region. One of the best things about living there was the amazing food. The strong concentration of several ethnic groups made that area a food haven.

One Buffalo delicacy is called *Beef on Weck*. It's a roast beef sandwich, served on a special roll called a *Kimmelweck* roll. A Kimmelweck roll has caraway seeds and coarse salt on the top, adding a nice crunch and flavor burst to the sandwich. The only problem is, salted rolls spoil very quickly (the salt crystals melt into the bread, causing it to become stale). If you don't use Kimmelweck rolls soon after they're baked, you'll need to buy new rolls.

That's what we mean when we say faith has a short shelf-life. Last week's faith won't suffice for this week's needs. When faith comes, you have a short while to act upon it before it leaves. Then, you'll need to get more; you'll need to hear again. The coming of faith is a continual process, requiring daily hearing. What happens to all our previous hearing, then? Is it worthless, like those stale rolls? Certainly not. Our months and years of past hearing combine to form a foundation of faith.

A FOUNDATION OF FAITH

We must differentiate between a foundation of faith and active, living faith. Both are necessary.

When a person comes to Christ, they often come with either no spiritual beliefs, or wrong spiritual beliefs. That person needs proper beliefs formed within them. As he or she hears the Word of God, beliefs are formed, creating a foundation that shapes the person's thoughts, words, and actions. This foundation is necessary, as it helps align a person's life with God's Word.

When the believer hears God's Word, faith comes. The hearing of faith does two things: it provides a supply of faith that can be acted upon at the moment, and it serves to strengthen the believer's foundation of faith. All scriptural hearing is valuable.

Even if we don't perceive a need at the moment requiring our faith, we always benefit from having our foundation strengthened.

A strong foundation of faith makes the hearing of faith an easier process. For example, I have been hearing for decades that it's God's will for me to be physically well. When I feed my faith in the area of healing, I am building upon those decades of foundational knowledge. My beliefs in this area are not easily swayed. I have fed my faith on the truth concerning healing for so long that you couldn't beat it out of me with a baseball bat. I *know* that it's God's will for me to be healed.

Even though I'm persuaded of God's will in this area, I still must continue to hear. It doesn't take much by way of symptoms or pain to challenge my belief that I am presently healed. I need living faith – faith for right now – to resist symptoms and pain when they come. I must continually hear in order to maintain my position as *the healed of the Lord*. Faith for my healing comes much quicker when supported by my decades-in-the-making foundation of faith.

We need both a foundation of faith and daily, living faith in every area of our lives. Faith must be developed in every area in which the believer receives from God. Since every person on earth needs salvation, all must hear about salvation. A person can hear about salvation one time, faith can come, and they can act upon that faith and be saved. However, they should continue to hear about salvation in order to develop a lifelong foundation in that area. After months and years hearing about God's plan of salvation, it will be impossible to dissuade them from the truth.

Let's speak of another area in which faith is required. The believer must receive provision from God on an ongoing basis. Therefore, a foundation of faith for divine prosperity is necessary. That foundation is set in place as the believer, day by day, hears God's Word regarding provision and supply. What happens once the foundation is in place? Can the believer take a break from hearing? By no means. Daily, living faith is still required. It's often the case that a person has a foundation of faith in place, yet hasn't heard recently enough to have faith for *now*. What must he or she do? Hear. It all comes from hearing. No hearing, no faith.

FAITH IN EVERY AREA

Every area in which God extends His grace is an area that must be met with our faith (everything He gives must be received). We must, therefore, hear from God in every area of our life. Since faith must be developed in each area, it's possible for the believer to have strong faith in one area while possessing weak faith (or no faith) in another. This disparity in believing is due to a disparity in hearing. When a person fails to hear truth in a particular area, faith cannot come. That person will, regrettably, have to do without their answer until they are able to hear.

For years, I had strong faith for salvation, but not much faith in any other area. I was in a church that preached about the salvation experience, but didn't recognize the truth of the Word in other areas. I had no faith for healing or prosperity, for example, because I didn't even know that the Word addressed those areas. Because I didn't hear, faith didn't come. Because faith didn't come, I couldn't receive from God. For years, I suffered and endured things that Christ had already suffered for me: things from which I had been redeemed. It's a horrible thing when faith doesn't come.

Finally (thank God), I began to hear the truth concerning healing. Faith for healing began to come and a foundation of faith was formed within me. A few years later, I heard about prosperity. Faith for provision began to come. My life changed for the better as I received from God in ways I previously could not.

A person can have strong faith in a particular area one day, but two years later have almost no faith in that same area. What happened? Faith left due to a lack of hearing. We must continue daily to feed our spirits upon God's Word. We must continue to hear.

Do you need healing in your body? Praise God, we have a Healer. God is our Healer as much as He is our Savior, but that truth means nothing to the many who have never heard of God's healing mercies. The mere fact that God is our Healer has never gotten anyone healed. He can heal any disease, but His healing power remains inactive if not received. Healing is received the same way salvation is received: through faith. How is faith for healing obtained? By hearing. To receive healing, a person must first hear about healing.

Pray for my cousin's healing. Such prayer requests are familiar to most Christians, but do you see why they are only mildly effective? Let's suppose I indeed pray, *God, please heal so-and-so's cousin.* What does that sick or injured cousin need? Healing. Assuming that he is beyond the help of natural medicine, he needs God's healing. That means he must receive from God. That means he needs faith; faith must come. That means he must hear what God has said in the area of healing. *Pray for my cousin* – sincere as the request may be – can help only to the smallest degree. There's more that needs to happen if the cousin is to receive healing. *He* must hear.

(There are times when we can pray and exercise faith on the behalf of others. For example, if a person is unconscious, not able to hear for themselves, it may be possible to exercise faith for them. We should not assume, however, that others will be able to use their faith in place of our own. In our life, we must assume the responsibility for developing our own faith. We must hear for ourselves. It's safe to say that if a person *can* hear, they *must* hear.)

If we must hear from God in order to receive, we must become familiar with His Word in the many different areas of our faith. Do you know enough of God's Word on healing for you to be able to feed your faith and receive? Do you know what the Bible teaches about prosperity? Many believers know little or none of the Word in these areas. If they don't know which scriptures apply to their situation, they won't be able to hear as they should. That's why faith doesn't come. That's why they don't receive.

The person who fails to take in God's Word will have no faith. No Word equals no faith. Little Word equals little faith. Much

Word equals much faith. When we hear of someone operating in great faith, we often attribute their faith to some divine gift. Not at all. Great faith simply means that person took in great amounts of God's Word. I'll say it again: much faith means much Word. People with strong faith have a large intake of the Word of God. There's no such thing as a person with strong faith who rarely hears.

Jesus spoke of great faith and small faith. Paul spoke of weak faith and strong faith. Faith can be found in people at different levels at different times. What do we know about these levels of faith? They are tied to one's intake of the Word of God. Little faith means there has been little hearing. Great faith means there has been much hearing. We cannot be effective with our faith – receiving from God as we should – unless faith comes. Faith comes by hearing the Word of God. That's the *only* way faith comes.

Chapter 6
Hearing

We know that faith comes by hearing from God, yet we must take time to understand just what the Bible means when it speaks of *hearing*. Bible hearing is not the same as human listening. The phenomenon of sound bouncing off one's eardrums does not constitute Bible hearing. More than just a physical act, hearing is also a spiritual act. The believer hears with the heart as much as with the ears.

Many Christians (even faithful church-going Christians) have never really learned to hear. Years ago, I came to the realization that, although I had studied, read, and attended services, I was not really hearing as I should. All believers must be taught how to hear.

The primary reason why people don't hear as they should is that they don't understand the Word as they should. I'm not speaking about understanding what's *in* the Bible as much as I'm talking about understanding the Bible itself: what it is and where it came from. If we don't understand and approach God's Word correctly, we will fail to hear as God intended.

And we also thank God constantly for this, that when you received the word of God, which you heard from us, you accepted it not as the word of men but as what it really is, the word of God, which is at work in you believers.

1 Thessalonians 2:13

We call the Bible *the Word of God* or *God's Word* because that's what it is: words from God. We must treat it as such, bringing appropriate reverence to the words we hear. If we approach God's Word casually, we cannot expect to hear in a way that produces faith. We don't lightly browse Scripture (the way we would browse a magazine). We must intently take in the Word of God, realizing that His written Word is no different than if He were speaking to us, face to face.

My spiritual father, Rev. Kenneth E. Hagin was fond of making this statement in his meetings: *The Bible is God, speaking to me.* He would instruct us all to say that to ourselves and then turn and preach it to those seated near us. What revelation! Many agree that the Bible is God-inspired, but agreeing with that and having a full revelation of it are two different things. Do you *really* believe that when you hear the scriptures you are hearing directly from God? Many would say that they do, but few actually do.

It takes discipline to correctly approach God's Word. Our mind will always want to take over and analyze, but that's not the way to hear from God. Notice how James encouraged believers in this area:

> *So get rid of all uncleanness and the rampant outgrowth of wickedness, and in a humble (gentle, modest) spirit **receive and welcome the Word** which implanted and rooted [in your hearts] contains the power to save your souls.*
>
> *James 1:21 (AMPC)*

The Word of God is to be *received*, not just read and dissected. This verse speaks of *welcoming* the Word: accepting it as-is. We must welcome the Word the same way we would welcome a beloved guest into our home. When our guest arrives, our home would already be prepared and we would say, *Won't you please come in.* Too many people stand at the doorstep of their heart arguing with the Word instead of welcoming and receiving it.

Just as we would prepare our home for the arrival of a guest, we must prepare our heart for the arrival of God's Word. This is one of the reasons why church services often start with a time of corporate worship and praise. Besides ministering to the Lord, the believer's heart is being prepared: tuned to effectively receive God's Word. The hearing that produces faith doesn't occur until the Word of God is received.

es what God gives. However, before God's bless-
ceived, His Word must be received. He has given
us this word. There is no gift from God more precious than the
gift of His Word. There is no privilege greater than the privilege
of hearing from Him. Faith comes as God's Word is received by
the believer.

Let's speak just for a moment about what it means to receive
God's Word.

FAITH AND FOOTBALL

When I pastored in New York State, we had a professional
football player who attended our church for a short while. He
was a young player at the time, just in his first year, but went
on to have a good long career. This man was a wide receiver. A
receiver in football has much in common with a receiver of the
Word of God.

Many people believe that a wide receiver's job is simply to
catch the football. That's true to a degree, yet by no means is
catching the ball the entirety of their job. Before catching anything, the receiver has another job: being in the right place at
the right time. The quarterback (who throws the ball) is going
to throw the ball where the receiver is *supposed* to be, not where
he might have wandered off to. It's the receiver's job to be in the
right place at the right time.

The Christian also must be in the right place at the right time.
Like the receiver, he or she must be positioned to receive. No,
they aren't trying to catch a ball, rather they must be positioned

to hear God's Word. One way that the believer can position him or herself to receive is by being sure they always make it to their local church to hear God's Word. It doesn't matter how good a preacher your pastor is if you aren't there to hear. God delivers your answers to your local church. Be there so you can receive.

The receiver in football endures great opposition as he executes the various plays that are called. Mean-spirited defensive backs cling closely to him with the purpose of preventing him from catching the ball. The believer, likewise, must understand that he or she has an opponent, the devil, whose goal is to prevent him or her from receiving the Word. Where does the devil begin his defensive onslaught? At the point of hearing. If he can keep the believer from hearing, he can prevent the Word from having any real effect.

> *The sower sows the word. And these are the ones along the path, where the word is sown:* **when they hear, Satan immediately comes** *and takes away the word that is sown in them.*
>
> *Mark 4:14-15*

As the wide receiver reaches up to catch the football, the defender swats at the ball, attempting to knock it out of the receiver's grasp and onto the turf. If the defender is successful, the result is the same as if the ball had never been thrown to the receiver. So too, if we hear but don't receive (hearing casually), the Word of God is rendered ineffective. Our lives receive the same benefit as if we had never heard in the first place.

The actual catching of the football is where our greatest illustration is found. The wide receiver, having sprinted to the correct spot on the field, leaps past the distractions of the defender and focuses solely on the ball. He catches the ball, grabbing it with both hands and bringing it down to his midsection where it can be safely tucked away. He then points his body in the direction of his team's goal line and makes as much progress as he can toward that goal. All the while, the defender is trying to pry the ball loose from the receiver's hands, stopping his progress. There's nothing casual or random about receiving in football. Receiving is hard work.

As the Christian hears the Word of God, distractions appear from every side, attempting to yank the Word away. The believer, like the wide receiver, cannot not sit idly by in a disengaged manner, but must actively reach out to receive God's Word. He must hold tightly to the Word, channeling it into his midsection – his spirit – where it produces faith. Then, he must begin to take steps, ordering his life in the direction of the Word, progressing toward the goal of his faith. The believer and the wide receiver indeed have much in common.

We must bring discipline to the spiritual act of hearing, much like the football player brings discipline to his sport. We must train ourselves to hear. How we approach God's Word determines whether we are truly hearing. If we give the Word our regular and full focus, God's Word will quickly penetrate our inner man, producing faith. Only when that happens – only when we really hear and are convinced of the truth – can we say that faith has come.

PAY ATTENTION

The hearing of faith is not difficult yet, at the same time, it's not easy. It's sort of like when a husband and wife want to have a meaningful conversation while several of their kids are in the room. The process of a deep conversation is not hard, but tuning out the many distractions and voices that are present can be a challenge. As a believer, it can be challenging to tune out the other voices that are vying for your time and attention. It can seem as though it takes faith just to get faith.

I love this passage in Proverbs, one of the greatest in the Bible along these lines:

> *My child, pay attention to what I say. Listen carefully to my words. Don't lose sight of them. Let them penetrate deep into your heart, for they bring life to those who find them, and healing to their whole body. Guard your heart above all else, for it determines the course of your life.*
> *Proverbs 4:20-23 (NLT)*

Notice this first phrase: *pay attention.* Had we nothing but these two words of instruction, we would have the key to being a true receiver instead of a casual hearer. How can we be sure we are hearing correctly? How do we know if we're positioned to receive? We receive when we give our full attention to God's Word.

We hear correctly when we pay attention.

If you received a call from your doctor's office, informing you that your doctor was concerned by your test results and wanted to meet with you, how would you listen? Would you sit there, mindlessly staring out the window or secretly browsing your phone? Certainly not. In a life-or-death situation, you would listen with the utmost intensity, hanging on to the doctor's every word, clinging to every ounce of hope. You would very likely take notes as he began speaking of possible treatments. Why? His words – any of his words – could change the course of your life. You wouldn't want to forget anything he told you.

Why do people listen so intently at a doctor's visit, yet listen so casually to the Word of God? Because they don't believe the Word of God to be nearly as important. They don't allow the preacher's words to have the life-changing impact of the doctor's words. This should not be. God's Word is every bit as important (much more so, in fact) as the word of the medical professional. It is indeed a matter of life and death. We must reject casual hearing, learning instead to intently receive God's Word.

Not giving God's Word the gravity it deserves is the reason why people don't listen as intently as they should. Many would never think of bringing a notebook to church. They don't really believe that God is personally present, speaking directly to them. If they possessed a revelation of the importance of the Word of God, they would sit on the edge of their seat instead of sinking back, drifting off to sleep.

For good news came to us just as to them, but the message they heard did not benefit them, because they were not united by faith with those who listened.

Hebrews 4:2

This verse reveals that it's possible to hear God's Word, yet receive no benefit. It's possible to hear, yet faith not come. If the Word is to benefit our lives, we must practice the kind of hearing that leads to faith.

People don't receive answers to their needs because they don't have faith. They don't have faith because faith hasn't come. Faith hasn't come because they haven't heard. Many haven't heard because, when God's Word was being preached, they weren't paying sufficient attention. We must give our full attention to God's Word, doing as Proverbs 4:20 says: *listening carefully.*

Many occupy seats in the church but allow their minds to drift elsewhere. They are thinking about what they will do after the service and are easily distracted. I have been in services where, if a person comes in late, the entire congregation looks to see who it is. They give no thought to the fact that they might miss some of what is being preached. Such people lack revelation of the importance of the Word of God. If they really saw the Word as their answer, they wouldn't care if the building was on fire. They would stay put, glued to the Word that was being preached until someone told them they had to evacuate.

PENETRATION

Proverbs 4:21 says *Don't lose sight of them. Let them penetrate deep into your heart.* The way to not lose sight of the Word is to keep it before your eyes on a regular basis. Verses that feed your faith and seem to help you the most should be viewed as often as possible during the day. Even if you can quote them, it's helpful to open your Bible and read them. Your physical eyes are a doorway to your spiritual eyes. Your physical ears are a doorway to your spiritual ears. Be a focused, purposeful hearer.

The result of paying attention to God's Word – keeping it in your ears and before your eyes – is that His Words will *penetrate deep into your heart.* This is significant. Heart-penetration is not just a symbolic phrase or thought, but an actual event. When our attention is fixed and our senses focused on God's Word, a pathway is opened whereby the Word of God can enter our spirit. Spirit-penetration is the goal of all hearing. Only when God's Word penetrates (gains entrance into) our spirit does faith come. Notice this familiar verse:

> For **with the heart one believes** and is justified, and with the mouth one confesses and is saved.
> *Romans 10:10*

The heart, or spirit, of man is the instrument with which man believes. Although the mind is involved, we can't believe God with our mind. This is an area of great misunderstanding. Many attempt to relate to God purely on an intellectual level. They think faith comes from being convinced of certain intellectual facts. Not so. Faith comes when the Word of God penetrates one's spirit. A person may or may not fully understand what they are hearing on an intellectual level, but when God's Word is received into their spirit, they will become convinced that what He says is so.

Faith is of the heart, not the head. Because many are naturally educated rather than spiritually enlightened, their intellect hinders faith rather than helping it. When people have been taught to be analytical and skeptical in their approach to everything in life, it's only natural that they bring that same skepticism to God's Word. This, however, is not the way to receive. What if the football player stopped to analyze the speed, trajectory, and shape of the ball before bringing it close to his body? There would be far fewer receptions.

Don't misunderstand me. God's Word can handle all the scrutiny we can throw at it. Even from an intellectual standpoint, God's Word holds up just fine. Yet, when we filter God's Word through our intellect, it rarely reaches the spirit. Believers must decide ahead of time that, if God said it, it's true. If it's in the Word, it's safe to believe, receive, and act upon. When you hear the Word, don't pick it apart with your mind. Just welcome it in with a wide-open heart. Later, after you receive it, your mind will understand.

Believers must train themselves to hear by focusing on what God is saying, receiving His words into their spirit as truth. When God's Word penetrates the heart, faith comes; the person has what they need to receive from God. The analytical mind, on the other hand, restricts the flow of God's Word to the heart. While the person is questioning and analyzing, the impact of the Word is lessened. Heart-penetration does not occur. Faith doesn't come.

Rev. Kenneth E. Hagin possessed great revelation along these lines. He developed the habit of proper hearing and urged others to do the same, knowing that the hearing of faith does not occur randomly or accidentally. In teaching others, Brother Hagin made this statement, which summarizes well the emphasis of this chapter and the emphasis of Scripture:

> *I had to come down to the brink of the grave before I'd do what I'm urging you to do—come to God's Word in a constant, careful, diligent, reverent, prayerful manner and find out what God's Word has to say.* *

May we, like Brother Hagin, learn to properly approach God's Word. May we discipline ourselves to hear and receive the Word as it truly is: the difference between victory and defeat, bondage and freedom, life and death. May we learn to hear.

*Excerpt From: Kenneth E. Hagin. "God's Medicine." Faith Library Publications.

Chapter 7

Healing

*My child, pay attention to what I say. Listen carefully to my words. Don't lose sight of them. Let them penetrate deep into your heart, for **they bring life** to those who find them, **and healing** to their whole body. Guard your heart above all else, for it determines the course of your life.*

Proverbs 4:20-23 (NLT)

This passage says *they bring life to those who find them, and healing to their whole body.* What does it mean by the phrase *they bring life*? *They* is referring to God's Word. His words are alive (Hebrews 4:12), bringing a flow of God's life to our life. Notice also that His Words bring healing. Many try to take every scriptural reference to healing and spiritualize it, saying that it's speaking only of spiritual healing. That's certainly not true here.

Physical, bodily healing is specifically mentioned.

His Words bring life to those that *find them*. How does one find God's Word? An index? The table of contents? A concordance? No, this verse isn't speaking of finding God's Word on the page, it's speaking of the words on the page finding their way into your spirit. You find God's Word when God's Word gets in you.

Many years ago, I was prompted to look up this phrase *find them* in the Hebrew. When I read the definition, it impressed itself upon my spirit; I have never forgotten it. *Find means to purposefully search, discover, get under the power of, and move in the direction of.* That's what we must do with God's Word. Purposefully search out the truths of Scripture. Discover their meaning. Get under the power of the Word, submitting your life to God's principles. Move in the direction of the Word. When we give the Word that kind of place in our life, the Word becomes to us a flow of life.

Having been raised Jewish, I remember the services that I would attend at our temple. One of the most solemn parts of the service was the handling of the Hebrew scrolls (the Torah). Those scrolls were not tossed about casually, but were carefully placed up on the platform in an enclave known as the *Ark* (symbolic of the Old Testament Ark of the Covenant). The Torah was protected with elaborate cloth coverings and silver-plated decorative ornaments (similar to those of Aaron's priestly garments).

There was a special ceremony to remove the scrolls from the ark and remove their protective coverings. A sense of awe prevailed when the scrolls were opened and God's Word was read. This was no casual affair but was, in some ways, the most memorable part of the service. If the Jews – those who embrace only the lesser blessings of the Old Covenant – can bring such reverence to the Word of God, shouldn't we who are further enlightened bring similar reverence? (Of course, our honor and care should be for God's words themselves rather than just the physical form of the book.)

MEDICINE

God's Word brings healing to our whole body. The Hebrew word translated *healing* could literally be translated *medicine*. God's Word is *medicine to our whole body*. What does that mean? It means that His Word will accomplish in us everything that natural medicine could accomplish (albeit without any side effects or limitations). This is an amazing truth; great news! Yet, we must understand exactly how His medicine works.

God's Word only brings healing power to our body if His Word gets in us. His Word only acts as medicine if we give it its rightful place in our life: keeping it before our eyes and allowing it to penetrate our heart. We must take in His Words. We must take our medicine if it is to work.

My wife worked for several years as a medical assistant in a dermatology office. One of her jobs was to note the treatment plan that the doctor had prescribed and make sure the patient understood that plan. At the patient's follow-up visit, my wife would read their medical chart and ask how the treatment was working. Often the patient would answer, *I'm no better.* The first question my wife would ask is if they had been taking their medicine as prescribed.

It was astounding how many of these patients would answer by saying they had not taken their medicine. They either forgot to take it, chose not to take it, or modified the dosage as they saw fit. Many thought they knew better than the doctor, assuming that his prescription wouldn't work. They were correct. It didn't work, but not because the doctor didn't know what he was doing. It didn't work because they didn't take it as prescribed.

Christians, sorry to say, are often no smarter than the patients at that doctor's office. God has given us His prescription for divine health, yet Christians refuse to take their medicine. They think that having the Bible on a table next to their bed will get the job done. That's as ridiculous as thinking that keeping your medicine bottle next to your bed will get the job done. Medicine, naturally and spiritually, only works when taken according to directions. It only works when it gets in you. God gave us His directions: His prescription. He told us to constantly approach His Word in a regular, focused, diligent manner.

If we take God's medicine as prescribed, it will work every time. His Words bring healing to our *whole body. Whole* means that no part is excluded. There is no sickness or disease – not one – that the life-giving power of the Word can't overcome. Medical science doesn't have an answer for every physical malady, but God's Word does. The Word will cure anything. Healing from every disease is available, but before healing comes hearing.

There are dozens of scriptures one could hear that will produce faith for healing. It's wise for the believer to know these different healing verses. Yet, God may lead the believer to just a particular verse or two as they are going through a test or trial. Just as a doctor knows the best medicine to prescribe in different situations, God knows exactly which scriptures will best address an individual believer's situation. He will lead us to the medicine that works best for us at the time.

All of God's Word is life and health to our flesh, not just the verses that speak of healing. We must understand that sickness is not always physical in origin; there are several ways it can arise. For example, a person can open the door to sickness and disease through disobedience, giving the enemy access into their life. In such cases, verses that encourage obedience would be the best medicine. God's Word brings light in every area of our life, helping us see where we may have missed it and guiding us toward any needed correction.

FOCUSING ON THE WORD

And the Lord said to Moses, Make a fiery serpent [of bronze] and set it on a pole; and everyone who is bitten, when he looks at it, shall live. And Moses made a serpent of bronze and put it on a pole, and if a serpent had bitten any man, when he looked to the serpent of bronze [attentively, expectantly, with a steady and absorbing gaze], he lived.

Numbers 21:8-9 (AMPC)

In this story, the Children of Israel had sinned. Their griping and complaining opened a door of access to the enemy, who afflicted them with poisonous snakes. All throughout the camp, people were dropping dead from snake bites. God, in His mercy, commanded Moses to construct a bronze serpent, set high upon a pole. This serpent represented the curse that was afflicting them. The pole represented the cross where Jesus, centuries later, would suffer and die, taking upon Himself the curse of sickness. To us, this story is a wonderful illustration of redemption. To Israel, it was life in the face of certain death.

Those who were bitten had to disregard the symptoms they were experiencing and instead focus on that bronze serpent. Although the act of staring at a pole is not, in itself, difficult, think about how difficult it must have been for the people to control their thoughts. Put yourself in their place. After seeing several people around you die from snake bites, you have been bitten yourself. Instead of watching your wound, you are to watch your redemption. Instead of looking at the problem, you are to focus on the answer.

The Israelites were to look at the serpent *attentively, expectantly, with a steady and absorbing gaze.* As they focused on the serpent on the pole, they saw their sickness judged and themselves set free. As they steadfastly continued their gaze, soaking in the power of their redemption, faith came and power flowed. Healing became a reality in their life.

How could faith come if they didn't hear anything? They did hear. When you stare into the pages of the Bible, you are hearing, even if no audible word is spoken. The hearing of faith occurs, not when words are spoken out loud, but when God's Word penetrates your spirit. This can happen by receiving the Word visually as well as audibly.

Israel was healed as they gazed upon the bronze serpent, seeing themselves free from the poisonous curse. We receive our healing when we see Jesus having taken our place in sickness, suffering the curse on our behalf. We gaze into the pages of the Word of God until we see ourselves healed. Then, God's Word penetrates our inner man. His healing power flows freely into our life, driving out sickness and disease.

HEARING AND HEALING

*But now even more the report about him went abroad, and great crowds gathered **to hear him and to be healed** of their infirmities.*

Luke 5:15

Although multitudes came to Jesus desiring healing, there was an important step that first had to occur. Before they could be healed, they had to hear. Hearing precedes healing.

Many desire healing, yet refuse to hear; they want healing on their terms, not God's. I'm sorry, it just doesn't work that way. Healing, contrary to the beliefs of many, is not something bestowed upon us by God's sovereign choice. We have a part to play. Although available to all, healing must be received. That means faith is required. That means faith must come. That means we must hear. We must come with a receiving heart, giving full attention to God's Word.

As wonderful as the Christian life is, it's not effortless. While others can encourage and assist our faith, they cannot assume our spiritual responsibility. Many fail to understand this. They say, *Pray for me* when they should be saying, *Teach me*. Although prayer has its place, we can't substitute praying for hearing. Christians must hear if they are to receive. Rather than hoping that God will just *do something*, we must receive what He's already done. We must learn the principles of faith. We must hear.

Jesus, in the very next chapter, continues His emphasis on hearing.

> *And he came down with them and stood on a level place, with a great crowd of his disciples and a great multitude of people from all Judea and Jerusalem and the seacoast of Tyre and Sidon, who came **to hear him and to be healed** of their diseases. And those who were troubled with unclean spirits were cured. And all the crowd sought to touch him, for power came out from him and healed them all.*
>
> *Luke 6:17-19*

It's easy to assume that power flowed from Jesus because He was anointed. While that's true, it's only one side of the equation. In order for God's power to flow, there must be both a transmission and a reception. We receive by faith, yet faith can't receive until faith comes. Faith comes by hearing. Before ministering God's healing power, Jesus took time to teach this crowd. Although Jesus possessed a greater degree of anointing than anyone before or since, He still thought it necessary that the people hear. Their hearing brought faith. Their faith received, causing the power that He was transmitting to flow into their bodies.

We often minister healing in a service without taking time to instruct the people. Even when such ministry is initiated by the Lord, the results can be minimal. The reason? People have not heard as they should. They come with wrong thinking and leave without having received. Pastors, who see their congregation most often, must teach their people how to receive, instructing them to lay hold of God's power by faith. It matters how we come. It matters that we hear.

And he said to them, "Pay attention to what you hear:
with the measure you use, it will be measured to you,
and still more will be added to you.

Mark 4:24

Jesus, here, is teaching that our level of receiving is connected to our level of hearing. Little hearing, little receiving. Much hearing, much receiving.

It doesn't just matter *that* we hear, it matters *what* we hear. We must be diligent to only hear good things, recognizing and rejecting doubt and unbelief. Only listen to preaching and teaching that brings faith. Much of what is featured on Christian television or radio hinders faith instead of helping it. Sure, we can find some good in almost every sermon, but when it comes to protecting our faith, we must become selective, feeding only on that which strengthens our inner man.

Notice Luke's rendering of this verse:

> **Take care then how you hear,** *for to the one who has, more will be given, and from the one who has not, even what he thinks that he has will be taken away.*
>
> *Luke 8:18*

Pay attention to what you hear. Take care then how you hear. The Word is clear that much depends on our hearing: the right kind of hearing.

Our hearing determines our future. Attentive hearing leads to blessing and increase. Casual hearing leads to subtraction and loss. Just being around the Word is not enough. A person can attend the greatest church in town and receive nothing, while others in that same church receive much. Who determines our level of receiving? We do. We determine what we receive – we determine the outcome of our life – by the way we hear.

Whether or not we are healed is up to us. Whether we prosper is up to us. It all starts with hearing. The casual hearer immediately forgets the Word that he or she has heard, their mind quickly moving on to other things. The purposeful hearer, on the other hand, retains what has been heard, immediately putting the Word into practice. Instead of forgetting the Word, they allow it to affect their thoughts, words, and actions. The Bible indicates that such individuals will enjoy God's best.

> *But the one who looks into the perfect law, the law of liberty, and perseveres, being no hearer who forgets but a doer who acts, he will be blessed in his doing.*
>
> *James 1:25*

Proper hearing means greater receiving. Greater receiving means more blessing. More blessing means more healing. If we see less healing today than in years past it's because there's less hearing today than in years past. This is tragic, especially given the fact that God's healing Word is more accessible than ever. We must become Word-people: focused, disciplined hearers with a voracious appetite for the Word of God. We must become like the followers of Jesus: those who came to hear and be healed.

Chapter 8

The Faith-Producing Word

We are emphasizing this phrase *faith comes*, for it was the Lord's emphasis to me on the night that He spoke to me. It's in this step, the hearing of faith, that so many fail. Because people may have heard the Word before, they assume that they know what it says and feel as though they can skip this step. They jump right in, trying to operate faith, but one cannot successfully operate faith without sufficient levels of faith. You can't use faith you don't have. You can't use faith that hasn't come.

How can we know if faith is present at sufficient levels? Wouldn't it be great to have a faith metering system? We do. Romans 15 reveals two indicators that measure the level of our faith.

*May the God of hope fill you with **all joy and peace in believing**, so that by the power of the Holy Spirit you* *may abound in hope.*

Romans 15:13

What do joy and peace have to do with the level of our faith? A great deal. Let's suppose, for example, that you received a letter saying that your monthly house payment was about to increase substantially. For most people, that's not good news. That extra amount of money every month, if not in your budget, can put you in a place of need. The prospect of an unmet need can bring feelings of fear and anxiety.

What does God say about your unexpected need? Philippians 4:19 says, *And my God will supply every need of yours according to his riches in glory in Christ Jesus.*

When you heard the verse above, what effect did it have on those feelings of anxiety and fear? Did the Word drive out the anxiety, replacing it with peace and joy, or did the Word have no real effect? For many, hearing God's Word in a time of need accomplishes absolutely nothing.

Many forbid the Word to have any real effect in their lives. They think, *That's something we look at on Sundays in church, but this is real life. This is our mortgage we're talking about.* In their minds, their circumstance is bigger than the Word of God. They want what they call *real-life solutions*, not just a collection of ancient sayings. Yet, when speaking to their pastor or others about their problem they might say, *We're believing God.*

Christians are fine with what the Word of God says until a circumstance comes along to challenge it. Then, they are quick to abandon their beliefs, looking elsewhere for solutions. They really don't see the Word as their answer and their help. They thought they were faith giants until their faith got challenged. No, they were just doing what everyone else in the world does: walking by sight.

You're not really walking by faith until you are presented with an opportunity to choose between God's Word and your circumstances. When you see the Word as your answer, choosing it over the circumstances, you've begun to walk by faith.

Let's get back to our mortgage letter and those accompanying feelings of fear. If you heard the answer in God's Word and were still filled with fear, we know that faith is not present at sufficient levels; peace and joy are not registering on your faith meter. That's not a knock on your spirituality, it's simply a fact that must be recognized and dealt with. What do you do now? If faith is not present as needed, more faith must come. How does faith come? By hearing.

Find scriptures (such as Philippians 4:19 that we read above) that apply to your situation and begin to read them. If you're alone or at home, read them out loud. Put the Word of God in your mouth. Let the scriptures play over and over in your mind, heart, and mouth. Remind yourself that God cannot lie. If He said it, He meant it. As you continue doing that, you'll begin to notice a change. Your peace and joy levels will begin to rise.

Look again at Romans 15:13:

May the God of hope fill you with all joy and peace in

> *believing, so that by the power of the Holy Spirit you*
> *may abound in hope.*

Inner peace and a joyful expectation are indicators that faith is present at sufficient levels. When God's Word penetrates your inner man, joy and peace will rise, overcoming the fear and anxiety you may have previously experienced. You breathe a sigh of relief as you realize that God is indeed bigger than your mortgage letter. You're aware that the peace of God is ruling in your heart (Colossians 3:15). You actually get happy as you realize that God knew about this need all along and has had a supply prepared to meet that need. Joy and gladness are erasing the wrinkles that had formed in your brow.

What's going on here? The scriptures brought joy and peace to your situation when they penetrated your inner man. You heard the good news and faith came. That faith can now be used: put into action. Joy and peace are the meters – indicators – that let you know that there's enough faith in your spirit-tank to use. If joy and peace are absent, faith hasn't yet come as it should. How do we fix that? Keep hearing. If you take in enough of the Word long enough, it will displace the voice of opposing circumstances and penetrate your inner man.

The reason why most never make it to the finish line with their faith is that most never actually start out in faith; their faith never makes it out of the gates, so to speak. Only the smallest percentage of believers feed upon the Word enough for faith to come. Many hesitate to even pursue the path of faith because when they tried to operate faith before, it didn't work. We can readily see why. Faith that hasn't yet come never works.

People who have heard the Word for years often wonder why circumstances still seem to be beating them up. Although beneficial to their foundation of faith, their past hearing isn't providing faith for their present circumstances. They must continue to hear for faith to continually be active. Faith must be present at levels that can be put into action. Faith for today doesn't come from yesterday's hearing. We must continue to hear. Faith must continue to come. How does it come? From an intent, focused hearing. What must we hear? We must hear the Word of God.

My spiritual father, Rev. Kenneth E. Hagin, received a commission from God to teach and demonstrate faith to the Body of Christ (an assignment which he faithfully fulfilled). When speaking of challenging circumstances in his own life, he would often say, *I don't pray about everything right away. I take time to build the Word of God into my spirit.* Why would a man who had been successfully using his faith for decades say that? Because he wanted to continue to successfully use his faith. He made sure that, before he used his faith, it was present at sufficient levels. We must do the same.

THE WORD IS ENOUGH

> But the righteousness based on faith says, "Do not say in your heart, 'Who will ascend into heaven?'" (that is, to bring Christ down) "or 'Who will descend into the abyss?'" (that is, to bring Christ up from the dead). But

what does it say? "The word is near you, in your mouth and in your heart" (that is, the word of faith that we proclaim); because, if you confess with your mouth that Jesus is Lord and believe in your heart that God raised him from the dead, you will be saved. For with the heart one believes and is justified, and with the mouth one confesses and is saved.

Romans 10:6-10

This is a classic passage, illustrating the simplicity of faith. The person of faith receives the Word without requiring accompanying physical evidence. If God said it, that's sufficient. We don't need Him to descend from Heaven to speak to us in person. He speaks to us in person every time we read His Word. Faith regards God's Word as equal to God Himself. Faith says, *Give me the Word and I'm good. Give me the Word and I'll readjust the entire course of my life.* For the person of faith, the Word is enough. The Word is all they need.

Notice this familiar passage from the ministry of Jesus.

*As Jesus went into Capernaum, a centurion came up to Him, begging Him, and saying, Lord, my servant boy is lying at the house paralyzed and distressed with intense pains. And Jesus said to him, I will come and restore him. But the centurion replied to Him, Lord, I am not worthy or fit to have You come under my roof; but **only speak the word**, and my servant boy will be cured.*

Matthew 8:5-8 (AMPC)

How many of us are content with *only* the Word of God as our answer? Does God's written word waylay all your doubts and fears, or do you not even look to the Word in times of testing? The centurion in this story, not even an Israelite, said to Jesus, *Your Word is all I need.* When His Word is all you need, all you need will be provided. When His Word is everything, you can have everything.

Those familiar with this story know that Jesus spoke His healing word right there: *Go; let it be done for you as you have believed* (that same word is true for us today). The centurion's servant was indeed healed. This is one of at least a few instances where Jesus ministered healing or deliverance without being physically present. God doesn't have to be physically present in order to bring His help to us. His Word is enough. God and His Word are one.

When the centurion responded to Jesus, saying *Only speak the word*, he uttered some of the most precious words in Scripture. This soldier was willing to lay aside mounds of natural evidence in order to align with the Word of God. I'm sure the Father's heart filled with joy at the sound of his words. I know Jesus was moved by them.

When Jesus heard this, he marveled and said to those who followed him, "Truly, I tell you, with no one in Israel have I found such faith."

Matthew 8:10

Jesus was filled with astonishment and wonder at the faith-response of this Roman soldier. We rarely see Jesus taken aback or overly impressed, but He sure was here. What impressed Him so? This man's honor for the Word of God. His revelation and conviction that a word spoken from afar would be every bit as effective as ministry conducted in person. May we possess similar honor and revelation. In the difficulties of life, may we say, *The Word is enough. Only speak the Word.*

Years ago, my wife informed me of a family member who had received an alarming medical report. When I heard the news, I stayed up almost all that night in prayer, begging God to act. The fact that the Word of God had already addressed this situation never occurred to me. In my mind, the Word wasn't enough, nor was normal prayer enough. I felt as though I needed to pray until God spoke to me audibly, preferably in vision form. This was a crisis! I wasn't about to believe anything unless it happened right then.

There are times when extended seasons of prayer are appropriate. However, my all-night prayer vigil was faithless. I should have done what Brother Hagin taught – take time *before* I pray to build the Word of God into my spirit – but I hadn't yet heard what Brother Hagin taught. Like so many others, I was doing all I knew, but I just didn't know enough. I hadn't yet learned to look to the Word as my answer. (God, of course, never did appear to me that night.)

Instead of praying to get our answer, we should get our answer, then pray. The Word is our answer.

But what does it say? "The word is near you, in your mouth and in your heart" (that is, the word of faith that we proclaim).

Romans 10:8

Faith penetrates the believer's heart as he or she hears *the word of faith*. I like that phrase. We could amplify it by saying *the word that brings faith*, or, my favorite: *the faith-producing word*. When we hear the Word of God with a humble, open, teachable heart, faith comes: the Word has free and full entrance into our spirit. If, on the other hand, we disregard God's Word, the flow of faith to our heart is restricted. Learn to feed your spirit on the Word of God, finding scriptures that speak to every area of your life.

We can readily see the significance of this phrase *faith comes.* The enemy, ever promoting ineffective, false versions of the things of God, loves when believers try to operate faith without actually having faith. It's like shooting a gun with no ammunition. You can pull the trigger and act like you're shooting – you can even tell people you went shooting – but if there's nothing in the chamber, you aren't really shooting. In the same way, people talk about how they're in faith, but it's often the case that they're just pulling the trigger of an empty gun.

One of my spiritual mentors, Dr. Ed Dufresne, shared a great illustration along these lines. He spoke of trying to use the remote control for his television when the batteries were dead. Because he didn't want to get up and find new batteries, he tried moving the batteries around in the remote to get a bit more life out of them. Then he'd go back to flicking the buttons, hoping that the channel would change. He was making the correct movement, but it was powerless movement.

That's exactly what many in the Body of Christ do. They go through the motions of faith without having their spiritual battery full of faith. They push the right spiritual buttons, hoping for change, but to no avail. Faith doesn't work unless faith comes. Faith comes by hearing. Hearing occurs when we take in the Word of God in a prayerful, careful, reverent, focused manner. Continual hearing produces continual faith as we take in the faith-producing Word.

Chapter 9

Strength

But in these things, all of them, we are coming off constantly with more than the victory through the One who loved us.

Romans 8:37 (WST)

We don't just want faith to be present, we want it to be dominant. We want to be strong – overcoming life's battles – overpowering tests and trials. When you struggle year after year with the same test, taking a small step forward followed by a big step back, you're not strong enough spiritually. (A strong spirit and strong faith are one and the same. Faith is spiritual strength.) This can be a frustrating experience for the believer, but there's hope. The test or trial wouldn't be in your life were you not able to overcome.

It may seem as though the test is greater than you can handle, but it's not greater than you and God. It's not greater than faith. You can grow stronger and endure longer, outlasting the enemy. Physically, we can't always develop enough to match an opponent, for not everyone's frame can support the same amount of muscle. The five-foot, five-inch, 130-pound man, no matter how fit, is not going to push back the six-foot-nine, 350-pound man. There are limits to our physical development.

Those limits, thankfully, don't exist in the spiritual realm. No matter our upbringing, race, gender, physical shape, etc., all can develop to a place of full maturity and overwhelming strength. We can grow stronger and stronger as we continue to develop our faith. How strong can faith become? Strong enough to lift and move the mountains of impossibility in our life.

Athletes can't take extended breaks from training and expect to perform at peak level. Their training must be ongoing. So too, believers must continually engage in spiritual training, feeding and exercising their faith (see 1 Timothy 4:8). If a believer wants to prevail, overpowering tests and trials, faith must come every day. That, of course, means he or she must, with an open, receptive heart, hear the Word every day.

It's easy to evaluate your own life and conclude that you're strong in faith, but self-evaluation in this area is often less than accurate. We may hear of someone struggling with a test or trial and think to ourselves, *I could do better than that. I'd just use my faith.* That kind of thinking is unrealistic. It's really hard to imagine what a test or trial is like. You aren't feeling the pressure of that trial or the severity of the symptoms. You're not dealing with the mental torment and the strength and force of the opposition like the person going through it. Truth be told, they may be faring much better than you, were you in their shoes.

(True people of faith are never critical of the faith of others. They know what it's like to be in a faith battle and know that, were it not for God's constant encouragement, they wouldn't have made it to the other side. The faith critic – and there are many in the Body of Christ – is a hypocrite who has never really used their faith for anything. Never criticize the faith of others. If you see someone struggling, add your faith to theirs. Help lift them up rather than pulling them down.)

We've all heard the phrase *armchair quarterback*. That's the person who sits in his easy chair, watching the game with snacks and beverage in hand, criticizing the athletes on TV. He makes comments like, *Oh my Lord, he was wide open!* That's easy to say from the easy-chair. You don't have defenders in your face and more about to close in from behind. I, myself, have watched players on television and thought, *I could do that.* Pretending you can do something and actually being able to do it are two very different things.

How would I find out if I could indeed compete with the pro's who play on television? I wouldn't find out on game day, for I would never make it to game day. If I somehow managed to convince a team that I could play at their level, they would bring me in for a workout where they would put me through some drills. During those drills, it would become apparent that I lack the skill, expertise, and fitness-level to compete. I would be sent home with instructions to dream about something else.

I can tell you how much spiritual strength a person has simply by putting them through a few drills. Church services, for the believer, are where these drills take place. If a Christian won't enter into praise and worship, for example, they just failed their first drill. If they won't receive or respond to the Word, they failed another drill. If they won't tithe, another fail. If their words are full of doubt and unbelief, fail again. Every Christian should become proficient in these spiritual exercises. They must master the faith drills.

Once you pass the faith drills you're going to have to face an opponent. The only way to really use your faith is to use it against something. Sports teams don't win games without an opponent. It's great to practice every day, but eventually you're going to have to line up against someone and find out if you're *ready for prime time*, as they say. It's great for Christians to practice their faith as they gather for worship, but there will soon come a test or trial, requiring faith to be put into action. You're going to have to fight with your faith.

> *Fight the good fight of faith, lay hold on eternal life, whereunto thou art also called, and hast professed a good profession before many witnesses.*
> *1 Timothy 6:12 (KJV)*

Notice that phrase *lay hold*. Faith is the spiritual strength that reaches out and lays hold of things. The weak believer unsuccessfully grasps for his or her desires but the strong believer is able to lay hold and possess what he or she desires. When faith has come it's like having teeth instead of just gums. Real faith can take hold and *hold fast*.

HOLD FAST

In superhero lore, there's a character named *Wolverine* who has metal spikes protruding from his hands. A person with strong hands can grab things, but the person with five spikes on each hand can do more than just grab. That person can *hold fast*, their spikes sinking deep into the object of desire. That's what faith is like when it lays hold. It sinks deep into the object of desire and brings it in. Faith can be so strong that there's no possibility of the item slipping away.

Many scriptures speak of the steadfastness of the believer's faith by using this phrase *hold fast*.

> *But Christ as a son over his own house; whose house are we, if we **hold fast** the confidence and the rejoicing of the hope firm unto the end.*
>
> *Hebrews 3:6 (KJV)*

> *As for that in the good soil, they are those who, hearing the word, **hold it fast** in an honest and good heart, and bear fruit with patience.*
>
> *Luke 8:15*

*And by which you are being saved, if you **hold fast** to the word I preached to you—unless you believed in vain.*

1 Corinthians 15:2

*Since then we have a great high priest who has passed through the heavens, Jesus, the Son of God, let us **hold fast** our confession.*

Hebrews 4:14

*So that by two unchangeable things, in which it is impossible for God to lie, we who have fled for refuge might have strong encouragement to **hold fast** to the hope set before us.*

Hebrews 6:18

*Let us **hold fast** the confession of our hope without wavering, for he who promised is faithful.*

Hebrews 10:23

Why so many verses encouraging us to hold fast? God wants us to understand that our faith will be opposed. Faith is always opposed. Were there no opposition, faith would not be necessary; we could simply walk by sight. The believer must learn to hold fast in the midst of the fight of faith. If I'm holding my dog's leash in my hand, folded up, I don't need to hold fast; no one is trying to take it away from me. But if I attach my dog's leash to my dog and take him for a walk, I must hold fast. My dog is strong and will try to pull me around the neighborhood.

Like a strong dog pulling a leash, opposing circumstances will try to pull us away from our beliefs. Strong faith stands firm, pushing aside the voice of the opposition. Weak faith, on the other hand, casts away its confidence and retreats. We must not underestimate the amount of spiritual strength necessary to win faith's battles. We train for this, hearing God's Word every day. We make spiritual preparation, readying ourselves for faith's fight. This kind of overcoming faith is spoken of throughout the New Testament, including this verse by Jesus:

> *Indeed, from the days of John the Baptizer until this moment, the kingdom of heaven is being taken by storm, and **the strong and forceful ones claim it for themselves eagerly.***
>
> *Matthew 11:12 (WST)*

JESUS' STRENGTH

Let's talk for a moment about Jesus' faith. How did He accomplish all that He did? By faith (which comes by hearing). He heard from God, becoming persuaded of the truth. Then, He acted on that truth, trusting the Father to take Him to the other side of every faith venture.

How did Jesus handle the adversity that came His way? Did He struggle for days, weeks, or months with the opposition that He encountered? He did not. When all hell came at Him in the wilderness, He prevailed, emerging stronger than ever. When

81

threatened by a monster storm, He overpowered it with peace. On several occasions, He forced death to loosen its grip on individuals, bringing them back to life. There was simply no defeating Jesus' faith. Jesus was strong: spiritually unconquerable.

Yes, but He was Jesus. Yes, He was Jesus: a man anointed by the Spirit. Whether facing situations in ministry or life, Jesus operated by faith. He had to hear from God before performing the miracles that He did. He had to draw out of the reservoirs of faith to escape the destructive strategies of the devil. Not once did Jesus succumb to the tests that came His way. Nor did He live a life of struggle. By faith, He steamrolled the opposition, winning every battle. If He won, we can win.

I believe it's God's will for us to develop in faith until we, like Jesus, are overpowering the opposition that we face. It's not God's will that we stay in the same fight year after year, never making progress, never winning our battles. We are wrong to think that the mere passage of time will make everything better. We err when we look ahead to next year and assume that all will be well. It's what we *do* with our time that determines whether next year will be better than this one.

The smart person develops their faith from a young age, giving heed every time they hear the Word. Throughout their life, they take time daily to keep themselves spiritually strong. When opposition arises, they double-up their Word intake, outlasting their opponent for as many rounds as are necessary. We must not be slothful and foolish, but rather wise and diligent. We must become serious about developing spiritual strength. The enemy will make sure that we have plenty of opposition on which to practice.

NOT STRONG ENOUGH

The book of Joshua tells the story of the Children of Israel receiving their inheritance. Although God had freely given them their land by His grace, they still had to receive; they had to take it by faith. One small issue was the occupants of the land, who didn't share Israel's revelation that the land had transferred ownership. God expected Israel to use their faith to drive out their enemies and possess what was theirs. Some of the tribes of Israel did just that, however, other tribes discovered that their faith wasn't quite up to the task.

> *However, they did not drive out the Canaanites who lived in Gezer, so the Canaanites have lived in the midst of Ephraim to this day but have been made to do forced labor.*
>
> *Joshua 16:10*

Why did Joseph's descendants (Ephraim) not drive out the Canaanites? They weren't strong enough. Our enemies will never pack up and leave as a courtesy to us. They must be driven out. Ephraim was strong enough to dwell in the land, living among their enemies, but they weren't strong enough to drive them out. The Canaanites, according to Scripture, live in the midst of Ephraim *to this day.*

Understand this: when the devil brings an obstacle into your life, he intends for it to stay forever. He knows he has no right to afflict a child of God, but that doesn't stop him. He wants to see if you will let him stay. Many believers adapt their lives to the enemy's strongholds instead of running him out. That's not God's plan but, in your life, you're the only one who can do something about it.

God has given us the spiritual resources to overcome every attack we might encounter. We must wield our spiritual weapons and win our battles. *I'm just trusting God to fight on my behalf*, some may say. Be careful with such statements. If you mean you're trusting God to do His part, supplying His power in response to your faith, fine. He'll do exactly that. If, however, you mean you're expecting God to take care of the situation without your involvement, good luck. Scripture is clear: dealing with the enemy is our job, not His.

If we fail to initiate action against the onslaught of our enemy, no action will be taken. Heaven will do nothing but say, *I wonder when he (or she) is going to wake up and do something about that.*

God told Israel that He was bringing them into their promised land. It was a land of freedom from oppression, a land of abundance and plenty, and a land of peace. It was to be nothing like the wilderness they had known, nor the centuries of slavery they had endured. Living side-by-side with people who were looking for the opportunity to slay them is certainly not what God had in mind.

Joseph's other son, Manasseh, also had an inheritance in the promised land. How did things turn out for Manasseh? Not much different from their close relatives, Ephraim.

> *Yet the people of Manasseh could not take possession of those cities, but the Canaanites persisted in dwelling in that land. Now **when the people of Israel grew strong**, they put the Canaanites to forced labor, but did not utterly drive them out.*
>
> *Joshua 17:12-13*

The Canaanites *persisted*. The enemy will persist in his attacks. He knows that most Christians will quickly give in, allowing him to stay. You and I must not be like most Christians. We must win our battles. Through faith, we can overcome every obstacle. God has already given us the victory by His grace. We must become strong enough in spirit to enforce those victories. We must become strong in faith.

Notice that when Israel grew strong they were able to secure a partial victory. Why could they not finish the task of utterly driving out their enemies? They had grown strong, but not strong enough. More strength was needed, yet they collectively stopped short of obtaining that strength.

As we grow in strength, progressing in faith, we will find that God allows bigger opponents to come against us. Be assured that, if they're there, we can beat them. We, unlike the Sons of Joseph, can win a complete and decisive victory.

No temptation has overtaken you that is not common to man. God is faithful, and he will not let you be tempted beyond your ability, but with the temptation he will also provide the way of escape, that you may be able to endure it.

1 Corinthians 10:13

Faith is our way of escape. It's our way out: the way to the other side of every battle. What if victory seems to elude us and the battle rages on? More strength is needed. That means more faith is needed. That means we must hear more. We must tune out other voices, focusing our full attention on God's Word. As we do, faith will rise in our heart, filling the voids of doubt and unbelief. Natural circumstances will fade to the background and we will move forward with confidence and boldness.

Chapter 10
Words by the Spirit

Although faith comes by hearing, hearing from God is not limited to the written Word of God. It's possible for God to also speak to us in other ways. He speaks to us by His Word and He speaks to us by His Spirit. Any word from God is a word by which faith can come.

When Peter asked the Lord if He could step out to meet Him on the water, Jesus said, *Come.* Until he heard that word, Peter had no basis for faith; no assurance that God's power would support him as he stepped out of the boat. *Come* was a word, not engraved on stone tablets or written in the pages of Scripture, but spoken directly by the Lord. We can receive similar words of direction today. Whether through the written Word or a word spoken by the Spirit, faith comes by hearing from God.

Several years ago, after having pastored for over a decade, I began to sense a change in my ministry assignment. Although many scriptures teach us how to pray and effectively serve God, none give us the exact coordinates for our next step in God's plan. We must discover His plans by remaining close to Him in prayer. After many months, diligently seeking God for direction, He spoke these words to me: *Get to Tulsa.*

I had lived in Tulsa, Oklahoma for several years while working for Brother Hagin. Tulsa is a great city, but at this time, having lived elsewhere for over a decade, I had no real desire to go back. In fact, my preference was to not go back. My preference, however, was irrelevant. God didn't ask me if I wanted to go to Tulsa, He simply said *Get to Tulsa.* He didn't follow it up by saying, *I'll be taking questions now.* This wasn't open for discussion.

I could have pretended that I didn't hear from God and just stayed where I was in New York. But since God's plan for me was to move to Tulsa, His grace for my life was now located there. Since our faith follows God's grace (receiving what He gives), I no longer had faith to stay in New York. God clearly told me where to go. The only way for me to operate in faith was to embrace what I heard and obey His direction. Faith for my life – receiving His health, His provision, His blessing – would work in Tulsa, nowhere else.

After several months living in Tulsa, the Lord, by His Spirit, dealt with me to leave and relocate to Colorado, where we have now lived for several years. His grace for my life moved to Colorado, therefore I had to move there. I had heard from God and faith came. Staying in Tulsa was not an option. Returning to New York was off the table. Colorado was it. I can't decide to move anywhere else and expect to be supernaturally sustained.

The reason many people don't move with God, keeping step with His plan, is that they don't have faith to accomplish that plan. They don't have faith because they haven't heard from God. They haven't heard because they haven't taken time to hear.

Just as hearing the written Word of God takes time, hearing from the Spirit takes time. We must engage in spiritual activity such as praying in tongues, worshiping, and praising if we are to hear from Him. It's important to note, however, that just because we *think* we need to hear a special word from Him, doesn't obligate Him to speak to us in some special way. God speaks to us by His Spirit as He chooses, if He chooses, when He chooses. Our job is simply to remain in position to hear.

Although God promises to lead us through life, He doesn't promise to speak *specific words* of direction to us. The main way that He leads us is through the simple witness of His Spirit (see Romans 8:16). That witness – His tangible inner peace – brings valuable direction to us, and is as significant as hearing His voice in any other form. His prompting on the inside is enough to change the entire course of our lives, and must be obeyed.

When God dealt with me to move back to Tulsa, He spoke on the inside of me with a distinct voice. When He later dealt with us to move to Colorado, it was by His inner witness. There were no spoken words per se, yet I knew just as assuredly that I had heard from God. That's how faith comes: by hearing. Whether through the written Word, a spoken Word, the prophetic Word, or the simple witness of the Spirit, God graciously gives us that which is needed to produce faith.

These leadings of the Spirit are a subject worthy of their own book, but I mention them here to emphasize the fact that faith can come, not just by God's writings, but also by God's leadings. When I sensed God's direction to move to Colorado, I, of course, continued to pray about it over the next several weeks and months. That witness – His inner peace – remained the whole time, yet He never chose to speak to me about it any other way. The witness of His Spirit is all I had because that's all I needed.

THE WORD FIRST

In discussing how faith comes, I mentioned words by the Spirit last, because so many people mistakenly put them first. I have dealt with many over the years who said with absolute certainty that God had told them to do this or that. I, also with absolute certainty, knew that they were wrong, that God *didn't* speak to them to do those things. How could I make such a statement? After all, I'm not God and don't know the details of their spiritual lives. Who am I to judge?

The reason I know when someone who thinks they've heard from God really hasn't is because I know the Word of God. The written Word of God always comes first. When someone says God told them something, yet the word they received doesn't align with the teachings of Scripture, I know they are wrong. They *thought* they heard from God, but didn't, for God never contradicts His Word. The genuine leadings of His Spirit are always in agreement with His Word.

We must understand that the devil can also speak to us, bringing us counterfeit leadings and words of direction. He attempts to deceive the believer by first speaking things that are in line with the Word. Then, once the believer is familiar with his voice, he will begin speaking things that are not in line with the Word. This is exactly what the devil did with Jesus in the wilderness. He used Scripture (albeit incorrectly) to try to get Jesus to listen to his voice, but Jesus knew the Word too well. Jesus could easily discern the difference between God's voice and the devil's voice because He was thoroughly familiar with God's written Word.

I'm reminded of a sad example along these lines. Not long ago, I was with a man who had recently given his life back to God. As I talked with him, I could tell that he was trying to hear from God, yet didn't have the necessary foundation of knowledge from the Word. The things he was saying God had told him were all at least partially unscriptural.

I attempted to help this individual but he wouldn't receive my help. The enemy – masquerading as God – was speaking to him, telling him to do things that, on the surface, seemed spiritual. He told him to fast for a few days. Then, he told him he wasn't praising enough. Those thoughts and suggestions were followed by other, slightly twisted but still mostly scriptural *words*. (Things that are *mostly* scriptural or *partially* scriptural are unscriptural and should not be acted upon. If a leading is from God it will be completely scriptural.)

Just a few days after I had spoken with him, I received a phone call that this man had committed suicide. I knew exactly what had happened. The same voice that he thought was God – Satan, disguised as an angel of light (2 Corinthians 11:14) – told him he needed to take his life and come to Heaven. Examples such as this serve to show us the necessity of putting the written Word first.

God can and does speak to us, leading us by His Spirit in various ways. However, any leadings we receive must be scrutinized by His Word. God's Spirit will never contradict the truths taught in His Word.

After God proclaimed this phrase to me, *faith comes*, I began to train myself in accordance with that Word. Now, every time I see the word *faith* in the Bible, I add the phrase *which comes by hearing*. For example: *This is the victory that overcomes the world, our faith (which comes by hearing). The righteous shall live by faith (which comes by hearing).* That helps me remember to do step one before moving on to step two, three, or four.

What situation presently exists in your life that requires faith? Has faith come? If so, great. Now you're ready for step two.

Chapter 11

Faith Says

And Jesus answered them, Have faith in God. Truly, I say to you, whoever says to this mountain, Be taken up and thrown into the sea, and does not doubt in his heart, but believes that what he says will come to pass, it will be done for him. Therefore I tell you, whatever you ask in prayer, believe that you have received it, and it will be yours.

Mark 11:22-24

The second phrase that the Lord spoke to me that night before bed was *Faith says.* Faith – believing and receiving from God – is more than just a treasure to be admired; it's a force to be used: put into action. I could have a garage full of high-end fishing equipment, but just having that equipment will never bring a fish into my boat. I must put that equipment to work. I must send the line out for a fish to come in. So too, we must send our faith out if the object of our desire is to come in.

Once faith has come, it must be put into action. Faith's primary action is saying. In the passage above, Jesus is teaching His disciples that if they will say what they believe, they will possess what they desire. He emphasized the *saying of faith*, yet speaking wasn't the first thing they were to do. Before using their faith, they were commanded to *have faith*. The hearing of faith precedes the saying of faith. We have it, then we use it.

This great passage, a hallmark passage on faith, follows an event that took place a day earlier. The previous morning, Jesus was in search of a bite to eat. When he saw a fig tree in leaf, He walked over, expecting to pull up a stool at the *Fig Tree Cafe*. Instead, He found the tree barren. Notice what happens next:

> And **he said to it**, "May no one ever eat fruit from you again." And his disciples heard it.
>
> *Mark 11:14*

The disciples had already watched Jesus do some amazing things. He had walked on water, cast a legion of demons out of the man of Gadera, multiplied loaves and fish (twice), calmed a raging storm, and healed every disease imaginable. In some cases, He spoke to situations that were miles away and got results as though He were physically present. That Jesus was master of His domain should have come as no surprise to His followers, yet they were particularly intrigued with this fig tree. Notice their response the next morning:

> *As they passed by in the morning, they saw the fig tree*
> *withered away to its roots. And Peter remembered and*
> *said to him, "Rabbi, look! The fig tree that you cursed*
> *has withered."*
>
> *Mark 11:20-21*

Peter was impressed that the tree, in the course of just one day, had died. He told Jesus, *The tree you cursed has withered.* Jesus' response was significant: *Have faith in God.* When Peter said to Jesus, in essence, *Look what you did*, Jesus' response was, *What I did, you can do.* Jesus' answer to Peter reveals that He did what He did, not by operating some divine gift, but by operating the principles of faith. He expects us to operate those same principles and receive the same results.

People often ask, *Why did Jesus curse that poor tree?* If we needed to know, God would have told us. The Bible only tells us that He cursed it, and it died within a day. Jesus did all that He did in obedience to His Father, therefore, He must have, in some way, heard from God. Let's learn from what the scriptures say and not be so occupied with what they don't say. Jesus emphasized the *how*, not the *why*. The *how* was faith.

The Bible says His disciples heard Him curse the tree. Why was it necessary for Jesus to curse it out loud? Because that's how faith works. Words, released into the atmosphere, create sound waves through which God's power can travel. This is how things have always worked with God. How did He create the earth? By faith. He spoke, power flowed through His words, and matter appeared where it had previously not existed. Faith, in action, has creative power. Faith causes the impossible to become possible.

> *By faith we understand that the universe was **created by the word** of God, so that what is seen was not made out of things that are visible.*
>
> *Hebrews 11:3*

Things from the unseen realm appeared in the seen realm after God spoke. We would say that *something* came from *nothing*. What if we, too, need *something* to show up where *nothing* has taken up residence? What if we need something to appear in the seen realm (or disappear from the seen realm)? We, like God, must speak words of faith. Having heard from Him, we must command things to be, or command them to go. This seems ridiculous to the un-renewed mind, but remember, it was Jesus who told us to have and use faith. We are to follow His example, applying faith to our mountains the way He applied His to the fig tree.

Words are vehicles through which God's power may be transported to a situation. Faith is the bullet in your gun, but words pull the trigger. Faith is the lure on your fishing rod, but words cast the line. Faith is the arrow on your bow, but words send it to flight. Too many hunting illustrations? Faith is the motor in your vacuum cleaner, but words are the switch that turns it on.

Without words, faith lies dormant. For faith to work as it should, it must be put into action through words.

THE HEART AND THE MOUTH

Because, if you confess with your mouth that Jesus is Lord and believe in your heart that God raised him from the dead, you will be saved.

Romans 10:9

In this verse, we see the two steps of faith of which we have spoken. First, faith must come *(believe in your heart)*. Then, faith must say *(confess with your mouth)*. If a person is to be saved, he or she must first believe in their heart that God raised Jesus from the dead. How does a person arrive at such a belief? Verse 14 tells us:

*How then will they call on him in whom they have not believed? And **how are they to believe in him of whom they have never heard**? And how are they to hear without someone preaching?*

Romans 10:14

We believe as we hear God's Word with an open and receptive heart. Look carefully at the 10th verse in this chapter:

*For **with the heart one believes** and is justified, and with the mouth one confesses and is saved. Romans 10:10*

We believe with the heart, not the mind. Just mentally agreeing with the Word is not enough; a heart-persuasion is required. The Word we hear must penetrate our inner man, bringing us to a place of conviction regarding Jesus' work on our behalf. Then, those convictions must be articulated – released into action – through words that proceed from our mouth. Faith is always found in these two places: the heart and the mouth.

A person, convinced of Jesus' lordship, must confess with *their* mouth that Jesus is Lord. No one can hear on behalf of another, and no one can confess on behalf of another. Each individual must express their own faith in Jesus' lordship. The result? Salvation. The person, spiritually speaking, passes from death to life. It's a simple but amazing process: hear, speak, receive a miracle. Hearing and saying. This is how we receive the things God has given.

Hearing is like depositing money in your bank. Saying is like writing a check or swiping your debit card. Having money and spending money are two different things. You need both – money in the bank and the means to draw upon it – to conduct financial transactions. Things you may need don't show up just because the money is available; you must put your money into action, initiating a purchase. Faith works the same way. You can have it in your heart, but it doesn't buy you anything until you spend it: initiating a spiritual transaction with your mouth.

God created the world with words of faith. Jesus performed the miraculous by speaking words of faith. Peter, Paul, John, and others all spoke faith-words that brought a flow of power on the scene. Like them, we must take our place as God's representatives on Earth, speaking words that align with His will and plan. Paul can't do your speaking for you. Jesus can't do your speaking for you. Your pastor can't do your speaking for you. *You* must put *your* faith into action with *your* words.

TWO WAYS TO SAY

In our text in Mark 11, Jesus told His disciples to *have the faith of God.* Then, He mentioned two different methods by which faith can be released into action.

> *Truly, I say to you, **whoever says** to this mountain, Be taken up and thrown into the sea, and does not doubt in his heart, but believes that what he says will come to pass, it will be done for him. Therefore I tell you, **whatever you ask in prayer**, believe that you have received it, and it will be yours.*
>
> *Mark 11:23-24*

Two forms of speaking are mentioned here: *saying* and *praying.* Faith may be released through either method, but it's important to understand when to use each method. Let's begin by talking about prayer.

When we pray, we are addressing our Father. Although prayer can take on many forms, we're speaking here of what could be called the *prayer of faith*: releasing our faith into action through prayer. What's faith used for? Receiving things that are not yet realities in the natural realm. When should we put our faith into action through prayer? When the things we desire are things that are received from God. If it's something He's promised – something He's made available to us by His grace – it's appropriate to release our faith through prayer. It's appropriate to ask.

Let's take the New Birth as an example. When a person hears the gospel and desires salvation, we instruct them to release their faith through prayer. That person may pray, *Father God, I see that I have sinned and need a Savior. I believe that Jesus is my Savior and receive Him as my Lord right now. Amen.* That person received: laying hold of what God made available and taking it to themselves. That's how to receive from God, by faith, through prayer.

Since we pray to receive what God has given, when do we say? Generally speaking, we say to remove obstacles in our life. Jesus said, *Whoever says to this mountain.* Things which seem larger than us and immovable (obstacles) may be referred to as *mountains.* Your mountain, no matter how large it grows or how long it stays, can be removed. You, however, are the only one who can move it. You move your mountains with your faith. First, faith comes by hearing from God. Then, you speak to your mountain, commanding it to move.

OUR AUTHORITY

Why must we speak to our mountains instead of praying about them? Because, God doesn't respond to the opposition facing us, we do. We can, of course, pray to receive God's direction regarding certain problems, but executing those directions is our responsibility. If the thief – the destroyer – has brought something negative into your life that needs to leave, *you* must do something about it. Remember, God's part is grace. Grace gives. God gives us His good and perfect gifts (James 1:17), but He doesn't stop the work of the devil in our lives. That's our job. We put a stop to the devil's work by speaking to the situation, commanding it to leave.

If something occurring on Earth is from the devil, it can only be stopped by someone on Earth with authority over the devil. What many don't fully understand is that each of us has authority over the devil's work in our own life. The one who *doesn't* have authority over the devil's work in our life is God. He doesn't have that authority because He has delegated it to us.

> Behold, **I have given you authority** to tread on serpents and scorpions, and over all the power of the enemy, and nothing shall hurt you.
>
> *Luke 10:19*

If I hire someone to do a job, I'm not planning to do that job myself. The fact that I delegated the responsibility to someone else makes it their job, not mine. Likewise, it's our job – not God's – to exercise authority over the devil in the earth. God simply won't do what He's authorized us to do. Besides, He doesn't live here on Earth, we do. As indicated in the verses above and below, our authority on Earth (supported by Heaven's power) is sufficient to hold back the enemy's work in our life.

I will give you the keys of the kingdom of heaven, and whatever you bind on earth shall be bound in heaven, and whatever you loose on earth shall be loosed in heaven.

Matthew 16:19

Why all this talk about authority? To help us know when to pray and when to say. If it's something we receive from God, we pray: we talk to God. If we need to deal with the devil, we say, speaking directly to the enemy or the situation. People often pray that God will rebuke the devil, putting a stop to his work in their life, but that's unscriptural. The only way God rebukes the devil in our lives is through our mouths. When the words we speak proceed from a heart of faith, God fills them with His power. Our words become His words, having the same effect as though He personally spoke them.

It's important to carefully define the scope of our saying. Some go overboard, focusing their faith and words solely on the devil, binding him from every imaginable situation. Notice, however, Jesus' instruction to us. He told us to say to the mountain, *Be removed. Be cast into the sea.* That's just a fancy way of saying, *Go.* No long conversations with the devil. No reciting a daily list of things from which he is bound.

When addressing the devil's work in our lives, we need say little more than *Go!* If your dog or your kids enter your house with dirty, wet feet and approach your carpet, you know exactly how to say, *Go!* You may even use another word: *Out!* It's not the amount of words that we speak that gets the job done, it's the authority and faith-fueled conviction by which we speak those words.

Remember what prompted this lesson on the saying of faith? Jesus spoke to that fig tree. He cursed it, forbidding it to continue deceiving people by advertising fruit where there was none. He didn't pray that God would kill it, He addressed it Himself. One short sentence was all it took. When addressing the devil or his works, we don't necessarily need loud volume, fancy words, or long sentences. Once faith has come, our words, filled with God's power, will get the job done.

Chapter 12

Faith's Confession

The *saying of faith* is how we release faith into action. It's also one of the ways we keep our faith active. To assist in keeping faith active, God has given us the spiritual practice of *confession*.

> *Let us hold fast the confession of our hope without wavering, for he who promised is faithful.*
>
> *Hebrews 10:23*

Many misunderstand what the Bible means by *confession*, for society's use of the word has been shaped by traditional religious thought. When we think of confession, it's usually in context of having done something wrong (confessing sins, or confessing to a crime, for example). We picture someone breaking down, reluctantly admitting to a priest, parent, detective, etc. that they have committed some bad deed.

The Bible's use of the word *confession* is much broader. Although the Bible does speak of confessing sin (see 1 John 1:9), that's not the main way Christian confession is practiced. The word *confess* literally means *to speak the same*. It's the compound Greek word *homologeo* (*homo* meaning *the same,* and *logeo* meaning *spoken words*). When we confess, we speak the same.

What does it mean to *speak the same*? We are to speak the same as God, our words agreeing with His. Confessing a sin, for example, means verbally agreeing with God about it. (When we confess a sin, we aren't informing God that it occurred. He already knows and sees all.) We come to God in repentance, committing to forsake the sinful behavior. We agree that it's sin. We align ourselves with His disdain for the sinful act and, with our words, move away from the sin and toward Him.

We don't just *speak the same* when we've sinned, however. We are to speak the same all the time, each day aligning our words with God's Word. When the Word contradicts natural circumstances, we choose to disregard the circumstances and instead speak the Word. The world calls this lying, however, it's not. Lying is a misrepresentation of the truth. Faith is the most accurate representation of the truth. Speaking what God says rather than what we see is an integral part of the *saying of faith.*

FAITH WORDS

> *Now faith is the assurance of things hoped for, the conviction of things not seen.*
>
> *Hebrews 11:1*

Faith deals with things *not seen* and *not yet*. When speaking words of faith, we speak of unseen things as though they were already *here* and *now*. Why would we say such things? Because God told us to and needs us to. He's the One who told us to *believe that we receive when we pray* (Mark 11:24). If we believe God hears and answers us when we pray, we should speak accordingly, talking about the object of our faith as though it had already manifested.

The Bible says *By His wounds we were healed* (1 Peter 2:24). When a person hears that scripture, faith for healing comes. The truth penetrates his or her spirit, producing an inner conviction that *we are healed*. That's step one of faith. Step two involves putting that faith into action through words. The believer might pray, *Thank You Lord that, according to 1 Peter 2:24, we were healed by Jesus' wounds. If we were healed, then I am healed. Thank God I'm healed now. I call myself healed!* In this case, a combination of praying and saying released the believer's faith into action.

These kinds of faith-words move our lives in the direction of those words. God inhabits those words with His power, bringing to pass their fulfillment. In the case of healing, it can take time for the natural realm to conform to the spiritual truth that *we are healed*; the body may continue to exhibit the symptoms it had before. What must we do while awaiting our full manifestation? We keep our faith active, continuing to speak in agreement with the Word. We keep saying the same thing. We confess God's Word.

Every time you think of it, confess God's Word over your situation: *Thank God, I'm healed now because 1 Peter 2:24 says, By His wounds I was healed.* This type of speaking is what the writer of Hebrews was talking about when he told us to *hold fast our confession.*

Look again at the verse we saw earlier:

> *Let us hold fast the confession of our hope without wavering, for he who promised is faithful.*
>
> Hebrews 10:23

Hope, in the Bible, means *expectation*: an inner excitement that accompanies our believing. The *confession of our hope*, therefore, is the *speaking of our expectation*. It's not enough to just have right beliefs in our heart. Those beliefs must also proceed from our mouth. Only then will spiritual progress occur. We are to *hold fast* – continuing, against all evidence to the contrary – to our confession. We are to continue to *speak the same* as our believing.

There will be plenty of opposition to your continued words of faith. That's why we are told to *hold fast*. *Hold fast* means *hold on*. Problems will try to make you let go of your beliefs. Natural circumstances will try to force you away from speaking the same as God. It's not natural to say something different than what is seen, heard, and felt. It's not normal to go against our physical senses. Faith, however, does just that. It swims upstream, continually defying natural evidence, giving God an open door to move in our situation.

When Jesus lived and ministered on Earth, He constantly spoke words of faith. Because His words were based on God's Word, God was able to attach His power to those words. God's will was fully performed through Jesus because Jesus spoke right words. What about God's will today? Is He ready, willing, and able to do the same things He did through Jesus? He is. He just needs words of faith to which He can attach His power. Who speaks those words today? That would be us. Jesus, Peter, and Paul aren't here to do it. We must speak faith-words: words that agree with God's Word.

TALK TO THINGS

Jesus didn't just speak to people when He was here on Earth, He spoke to things. He cursed a fig tree, calmed a storm, and rebuked a fever. These things responded to the sound of His voice because His voice carried God's power. Things will likewise respond to our voice. I believe there's a truth here that not many have seen. No, we don't randomly speak off the top of our head, frivolously claiming everything we see. We speak what God has said. We must be proactive in this area, putting words of faith into play. It matters how we speak. Don't just talk about the problem, talk about the answer. Don't say what it looks like, say what it's supposed to be.

Not long ago, while walking through my neighborhood, I stopped to look at a home that was being built. I noticed, laying on the ground, a pile of lumber that had recently been delivered.

When I looked at that bundle of 2 x 4's, the Spirit of God spoke to me and said, *Do you see that wood?* Although that's all He said, I instantly understood what He meant. He was reminding me of the fig tree Jesus cursed and how it responded to Him.

Jesus spoke to a tree and it obeyed. That means the tree could hear. If trees can hear, wood can hear (wood comes from trees). Just as Jesus spoke to that tree and it obeyed, things will obey our voice. As I walked back to my house, I realized that underneath all the stone, stucco, drywall, and paint are sticks of wood. That wood hears my voice when I speak words of faith. My house will obey me. Houses can hear.

I have important things to say to my house. First of all, I call it *paid for*. I like to say it this way: *My house is paid up, paid off, and finished out.* I say that almost every day. Why? Because that's what I want to come to pass. Those words are in agreement with God's will for my life, therefore, God can attach His power to my words. Many trip over the thought of speaking to things, their mind deeming the practice silly or ignorant, yet this simple principle works powerfully.

Brother Joel, do you really believe your house hears? You bet I do. If a tree, storm, fever, or mountain can hear, a house can hear. Jesus is the one who told us, in unmistakable language, that we can speak to things and expect them to obey.

And the Lord said, "If you had faith like a grain of mustard seed, you could say to this mulberry tree, 'Be up-

rooted and planted in the sea,' and it would obey you.

Luke 17:6

When God attaches His power to the words I speak, those words affect the natural realm where material things exist. We can talk to things and they will obey. We can call things that God has given us into our life and they will come. Every Christian (not just specially anointed ministers, but every believer) can call things that they need into their life and can command opposing circumstances to leave their life. Just as we would train a dog to respond to our voice – coming when we call him or leaving when we dismiss him – we are to use words of faith to call things into our life or remove them from our life.

We see God, in creation, calling things into existence, the creative power of His words causing matter to appear in the natural realm. We see Adam, in the garden, naming the animals, presumably so they would respond to the command of His voice. Jesus, on multiple occasions, altered the course of nature through the use of words. Joshua spoke to the sun and moon and they stood still. Anything that God has created – animal, vegetable, mineral, or otherwise – will respond to words of faith.

I've endeavored to faithfully practice this law of saying. It works. I've seen houses come and mortgages go. I've seen physical ailments depart. I've watched the plan of God come to pass. I've practiced this in my life for years and will continue to do so. Jesus saw things happen as He spoke. We, too, will see things happen as we speak. The things that are in your life can hear. Speak to them.

CALL IT

> *As it is written, I have made thee a father of many na-*
> *tions, before him whom he believed, even God, who*
> *quickeneth the dead, and **calleth those things which be***
> ***not as though they were.***
>
> *Romans 4:17 (KJV)*

God brings things to pass through words of faith, calling things that are not as though they were. If we wish to successfully operate in faith, we must follow His example. We must learn to call things that be not as though they were. Do you need more customers for your business? Call them in. Do you need more people in your church? Call them in. Do you need more money to sow? Call it in. Do you need favor with city officials to complete a certain project? Call it done. Call those things that be not as though they were.

Some, attempting to practice this verse, do so with a subtle variation that strips faith of its power. Instead of calling things that are *not* as though they *were*, they call things that *are* as though they are *not*. If they're struggling with debt, they say, *I have no debt.* If they're dealing with sickness, they may say, *I have no sickness.* Their confessions, although well-intentioned, are missing the mark. A slight adjustment in their saying will better align them with Scripture, positioning them for greater results.

When we voice our beliefs, our own spirit hears the words we are saying and is influenced. However, when we confess what we *don't* have – let's use the statement, *I have no pain* as an example – our heart is hearing the key word *pain*. Instead of calling things that are (the pain) as though they're not, it would be better to align with Scripture, calling things that are not (in this case, healing) as though they were. Instead of saying *I have no pain*, say *I'm healed. I'm free.* Now what is your spirit hearing? Healing. Freedom. Faith can come from those words.

The confession of our faith should proceed from a heart of confidence rather than a shaky foundation of fear. People, frantically trying to confess their problems away, unknowingly voice their fears instead of faith. To continually say, *I have no cancer* shows that a person is disease-minded rather than Word-minded. Such confessions reflect denial of the problem rather than persuasion of the answer. Focus on the answer. Speak the answer. Faith says, *My body is healed. My bills are paid. I am redeemed.* Healed. Paid. Redeemed. That's what we want to focus on; that's the truth we want carved upon our heart.

ANSWER THE PROBLEM

Faith doesn't ignore the challenges of life, it faces them head on. When David went out to face the giant, Goliath, Goliath began listing the many reasons why David should back off and run away. David, in turn, listed the many reasons why their conversation was about to be over. Instead of running away, David ran toward him, knocked him down, and cut off his head. Like David, faith runs toward its giants, knocks them down, and cuts off their head. When situations and circumstances talk to you, threatening your demise, answer them like David did. Talk right back to negative voices, replacing the voice of the opposition with the voice of God's Word.

Notice this translation of Mark 11:14, the account of the fig tree:

> **And answering, He said to it,** *Hereafter forever, from you no one eats fruit. And His disciples were listening.*
> *Mark 11:14 (WST)*

This verse says Jesus answered. Whom did he answer? The fig tree. That tree was talking to Him, telling Him He would have to go without food for the day. His body, already hungry and weak, was probably talking to Him as well. Things were talking to Jesus and He did the right thing. He talked right back. He answered.

Brother Joel, now you've really lost it. First you talk about us talking to things. Now you're talking about things talking to us.

Absolutely. Bills can talk to you: *You're never going to pay me off. I'm staying in your life forever.* Your body can talk to you: *You're not getting any younger. See all those wrinkles?* Your emotions can talk to you: *No one appreciates you at this church. The pastor doesn't recognize your gifts.* Circumstances of all kinds can talk to you. Don't listen to them, answer them! Interrupt them mid-sentence if need be. If you don't purposely talk back, contradicting the voice of your feelings with words that reflect God's Word, you will begin to conform, agreeing with the problem and disconnecting from your answer.

Years ago, God gave me a song along these lines called *Answer It:*

Answer the problem, answer the lack
Answer the symptoms when they try to attack
When things talk to you it's time to talk right back
It's amazing what will happen when you open your mouth
And you answer it

VAIN REPETITION

Another common error where confession is concerned is the belief that we must confess the Word a certain number of times before God will hear and answer. Jesus addressed this in His teaching on prayer:

> *And when you pray, do not heap up phrases (multiply words, repeating the same ones over and over) as the Gentiles do, for they think they will be heard for their much speaking.*
>
> *Matthew 6:7 (AMPC)*

The idea that we must log a certain number of confessions each day is based in fear and superstition, not faith. This practice is akin to the Catholic practice of repeating the *Hail Mary* prayer. It's what the *King James Version* calls *vain repetitions.*

> *But when ye pray, use not **vain repetitions**, as the heathen do: for they think that they shall be heard for their much speaking.*
>
> *Matthew 6:7 (KJV)*

Repetition in itself is not wrong. It's actually helpful. The problem arises when repetitions are vain. *Vain* means *empty*. Confessions, for the believer, are empty when not spoken from a heart of faith. You can fire an empty gun as many times as you want, but repeatedly pulling the trigger doesn't cause a bullet to magically appear in the chamber. Before confessing your desires, take time to feed on God's Word. Load your faith-gun before firing it. Then faith will come and your words will be filled with purpose and power.

Many believe that God acts on our behalf based on the number of times we pray or confess. Real faith, however, understands that God, in redemption, has already acted on our behalf. He's already provided all our needs. He's already pronounced us healed. Our confession is not for the purpose of convincing God to act, but rather to convince us to hold fast to our belief that He has already acted.

The believer who understands the power of his or her words can become powerful in the earth. We don't need empty, vain repetition, but rather words of conviction, fueled by faith. When we hear, God's Word penetrates our spirit. Faith comes. Then, *our* words penetrate the spirit realm, opening a channel through which answers, blessings, and miracles can flow. Learn to speak, not randomly or fearfully, but purposefully and powerfully. Your words will move mountains. Your words will create your reality. Your words work.

Chapter 13

Faith Moves

Once faith has come, it must be released through words. Then, we must continue to speak, holding fast our confession by keeping our words aligned with God's Word. But what comes next? Is that all there is to faith? No. There's more.

The Spirit of God spoke four phrases to me that night as I laid down for bed. The first was *Faith comes*. The second, *Faith says*. The third phrase He spoke to me was *Faith moves*.

Once we have obtained faith and released it into action through words, we must be sensitive to any further instructions God may give. Actions – movement in line with our believing and saying – are an essential part of the process of faith.

We've already spoken of the hearing of faith and the saying of faith; we could call this step *the obedience of faith*. When God requires our faith to be accompanied by acts of obedience, we must perform those acts. We must obey.

Abraham, often called *the Father of Faith*, didn't just believe and say. He also had to obey, climbing Mount Moriah to offer his son, Isaac. Noah didn't just receive the word of the Lord concerning the coming flood, he had to fire up his air compressor, charge the batteries on his power tools, and get to work. Moses didn't just confess away the waters of the Red Sea, he had to make movement, lifting his rod to part the water. Joshua and his followers didn't just release faith from their mouths regarding Jericho, they marched around the city, day by day, as instructed.

Jesus' ministry, although powerful in word, was also action-packed. There were times when He *spoke the Word only* (Matthew 8:8), but there were also times when He required specific action from the recipients of His ministry. *Stretch forth your hand. Go wash in the pool of Siloam. Go show yourselves to the priest. Make the people sit in groups of fifty.* Why all this movement? What's so important about action? In each case, the required action brought forth the desired results. God's power attached itself to the believer's acts of faith.

God will direct you toward certain action at times, leading you to victory. We must obey, giving our full effort in the direction of His leading. However, we need not wait for a special word or leading to begin to act. What is it that you're believing for? What has the Word promised you? What have you been saying? If you can answer these questions, you can answer this next question: what can you begin to do – what action can you take – that aligns with your beliefs?

Do you believe you're well? Have you been calling yourself

well? Then begin making movement, to the degree you are able. How would a well person act? What would a well person be doing? Faith – real faith – makes plans based on the Word of God rather than circumstances. Do you really believe you're well? Then plan accordingly. Meet your friend for coffee, go to church, get ready for work. Even if you can't stay as long as you'd like, your actions – the movement of your faith – will be something God can inhabit with His power.

I'm reminded of two great examples along these lines. One is the story of the Presbyterian minister, A.B. Simpson. Rev. Simpson had developed a heart condition from which doctors said he would never recover. That condition worsened until Brother Simpson could no longer fulfill his ministerial duties. He realized that, since the doctors couldn't help him, any further help would have to come from God.

(It's important to note that faith is not incompatible with natural remedies such as doctors and medicine. God is the one who has given doctors their ability to help us in our areas of need. However, the believer should look to God and His Word first. Seek God before you go to the doctor, and then seek His counsel as you consider the doctor's counsel and recommendations. Any interaction with doctors and/or medications should be accompanied by faith.)

Brother Simpson took time apart to seek God's Word on the subject of healing. What he discovered astounded him. He saw that God provided healing through Christ just as He had provided salvation through Christ. He also saw that, just as he had received Christ as Savior, he must receive Him as Healer. What was happening here? As Rev. Simpson heard from God, faith came. What's the next step? Faith in one's heart must be released into action through the mouth.

Brother Simpson actually wrote down the words that he spoke that day. To him, they were covenant words: sacred and binding. He said, *On this day, I receive Christ as my Healer. Therefore, I'm healed, not just from heart disease, but from every disease.* What happened when he released his faith? God attached His power to his words, bringing to pass the healing that Jesus had provided. How did things look from the natural standpoint? How did he feel? Likely, not much different.

Let's be clear: faith does not mean that everything in the natural will change instantly. If it did, the many encouragements to *hold fast* in Scripture would be unnecessary. Things certainly can change quickly in response to faith but, more often than not, our answer manifests over time. Don't forget this important truth. Storms and tests don't last forever, but neither do they last just a few minutes. How long a test or trial lasts depends on a variety of factors. The biggest factor? Your faith. Your hearing, believing, saying, and acting.

Brother Simpson – healed as far as he and God were concerned – began to minister again. He preached, enthusiastically sharing his newfound revelation of the healing mercies of God. His condition improved, but by no means was he symptom-free.

One day, while fellowshipping with some other ministers at a retreat, Brother Simpson was asked to join them on a mountain hike. His first thought was, *I can't do that. The doctors said I might drop dead if I exert myself like that.* Then, he remembered scriptures such as Matthew 8:17, *He took our illnesses and bore our diseases.*

If Jesus took them, Brother Simpson reasoned, *I don't have them. If I don't have them, I'm well. If I'm well, what's preventing me from hiking up a mountain?* Before he realized it, he had answered his ministry colleagues, *Sure, I'll come along.*

He testified that he felt as though he might die on that trip up the mountain. As he focused on the erratic beating of his heart, his condition worsened. When he turned his thoughts to the Word of God, however, his condition improved. Climbing that mountain was a battle, yet the battle was not merely physical. It was also mental and spiritual. For him to win the physical battle, He had to first win the battle raging in His mind. He had to ignore the voice of his symptoms, focusing his thoughts upon the Word of God. He had to keep moving up the mountain, empowered by the truth of God's Word.

By the time Brother Simpson reached the summit of that mountain, his heart was beating normally. He was completely and forever free from that debilitating condition. How did He receive his healing? By faith. Faith had to come (and continue to come). Faith had to say (and continue to say). And, faith had to move. Actions that corresponded with his beliefs were required. I'm convinced that, had Brother Simpson not climbed that mountain, he would not have received the full manifestation of his healing. Manifestation meets movement.

Some may hear that story and think, *When Brother Simpson proved to God that he believed by climbing the mountain, God healed him.* That's incorrect. He wasn't trying to prove anything, or get God to do anything. He climbed that mountain, not to get healed, but because he already was healed. God didn't heal him on top of that mountain, God healed him centuries earlier on Mount Calvary (when Jesus bore our sickness). His climbing the mountain – the action that followed his faith – simply opened the door for more of God's healing power to flow, driving out the remainder of the disease.

The great preacher, Smith Wigglesworth, so convinced of the necessity of faith's actions, would pace the platform at his meetings, repeating the phrase, *Faith is an act.* He understood that no action meant no receiving. Action – the movement of faith – leads to manifestation. Remember the ten lepers of Luke 17? As they went – as they moved – they were healed. We must be bold to move. We must be bold to act.

The other example that I was reminded of is the story of the healing of my spiritual father, Rev. Kenneth E. Hagin. He had been afflicted (also with a heart condition) his whole life, unable to enjoy his childhood. Just prior to his sixteenth birthday, he became totally bedfast. While on the bed of sickness, he began to search God's Word for answers. He (like Brother Simpson) knew that his help was with God, for medical science could offer no cure.

Brother Hagin read the account of the woman in Mark 5 who had suffered for twelve years with a blood disorder. Jesus spoke

to this woman, saying, *Daughter, your faith has made you whole.*
As Brother Hagin read those words, the Spirit of God spoke to
him: *If her faith made her whole, your faith can make you whole.*
If her hearing, saying, and moving brought her results, his hearing, saying, and moving could bring him results. God was teaching Brother Hagin that his healing depended on his own faith
more than on any other factor.

As he continued to read through Mark's gospel, he came to the
eleventh chapter, the passage where Jesus cursed the fig tree and
taught His followers the principles of faith. As he read, the Holy
Spirit called his attention to the last part of the 24th verse:

> *Therefore I tell you, whatever you ask in prayer,* **believe**
> **that you have received it, and it will be yours.**
>
> *Mark 11:24*

The Spirit showed Brother Hagin that we must believe we receive *before* we have. In other words, we must believe that our
answer is a present reality in our life before it ever shows up in
the natural. This is key. We must *have it* spiritually before we
have it naturally. We must have it inwardly before we have it out-
wardly. We must *have it* before we have it. Many who set out in
faith miss it right here, failing to believe they receive. Their faith
stalls because they don't believe they have their answer *now*.

GOD'S GONNA DO IT

The Body of Christ is in need of greater revelation in this area of believing we receive. One phrase we often hear faith-people say is *God's gonna do it*. There are many variations to this phrase, such as, *I believe God's going to heal me. I believe He's going to supply my need. He'll come through just in time. He's going to answer our prayers. God will take care of it. He's about to do something great. He's going to pour out a blessing. He's getting ready for something wonderful. He's about to do a miracle.*

These phrases all sound faith-infused but, in reality, they reveal a lack of understanding about faith. They all speak of what God is *going*, or about, to do. They speak to the future, whereas real faith is always *now*. When these kinds of phrases are spoken publicly, crowds usually cheer in delight. I, however, inwardly cringe, knowing that deferred faith is ineffective faith. Sure, God's works tomorrow will be as great as His works today, but faith is all about what we have now. (Say it a few times: *Faith is now.*) Individuals who are always talking about what God is *going* to do lack revelation concerning what He's already done.

This may seem like a subtle or minor issue – like I'm being overly technical or critical – but this kind of talk is one of the biggest indicators that a person who *thinks* they're in faith really isn't. Even great people of God can miss it in this area. A person with real faith simply isn't waiting on God. Stop talking about what we're *going* to see. If you don't see it *now* (in your believing, thinking, and speaking), you won't see it later.

The devil doesn't mind you believing God, as long as you never reach the place where you have it *now*: where you presently possess the object of your belief. Satan loves that song from the musical *Annie* that says, *Tomorrow, tomorrow, I love ya tomor-row. You're always a day away.* As long as faith is deferred – a day away – anything but right now – the enemy knows that he's safe. He knows that future-faith is failed faith.

If you're waiting on God to do something (whatever it is you need), you don't believe you've received it. If you don't believe you've received it, you're not in faith. If you're not in faith, God can't bring His power to your situation. If God can't bring His power to your situation, you'll have to make do on your own. I don't know about you, but I'm in trouble without God's power and help. I can't make it on my own. I must believe I receive. I must be persuaded that I have my answer now.

Brother Hagin saw this truth. He said, *I see. I need to believe I'm well while my heart is still beating erratically.* He made the adjustment, aligning his beliefs with God's Word, and began to thank God that he was already healed. After just a few minutes praising God, the Spirit spoke to him, saying, *Get up. Well people ought to be up at ten o'clock in the morning.* Brother Hagin, at that time, was almost completely paralyzed, but when God says *Get up,* faith moves.

He made movement the best he could in response to the Spirit's command. Although he only had limited use of his hands, he wrapped them around his bedpost, wiggling his way to a seated position. He then slid his legs off the bed and onto the floor. He said they dropped to the floor like two chunks of wood. He pulled himself up by the bedpost and began to praise God that he was – not going to be, but already was – healed. As he held on to that bed, praising God, something that felt like warm honey hit him in the head and ran down his body (that was the anointing: the power of God). The next thing he knew, he was standing up without assistance, healed.

What happened? Brother Hagin's cooperation with the laws of faith – hearing, saying, acting – gave God an open channel through which His power could flow. But what if he hadn't acted? What if, when God told him, *Get up*, he reasoned it away, saying, *I'm paralyzed*, or, *I'm too weak for that?* He wouldn't have received the manifestation of his healing had he not obeyed. His obedience – the action of his faith – opened the door for God's power to flow. The flow of God's power moved his healing from the spiritual realm to the natural realm where it could be experienced physically. God moved by His power because Brother Hagin moved in faith. Faith moves.

Chapter 14

Corresponding Actions

What good is it, my brothers, if someone says he has faith but does not have works? Can that faith save him?

James 2:14

Having faith is important. It's the first step in seeing impossible situations come to pass. But having faith is not the only step. Faith doesn't just come, it also says and moves. James, in this verse, asks the question, *If faith is not accompanied by works, can faith save?* In other words, if someone has faith but doesn't put it into action, will his or her faith work? The answer is a resounding *no*.

This verse has always required explanation due to the words *works* and *save*. Many assume that *works* is the same as the works of the law (the efforts of the flesh). That's not the case here. *Works* is simply referring to actions that correspond to our beliefs. The word *save*, contrary to common belief, is not just speaking about coming to Christ and being born again. Salvation, in the New Testament, includes everything the believer would receive from God.

The Weymouth Translation brings much-needed clarity:

> *What good is it, my brethren, if a man professes to have faith, and **yet his actions do not correspond**? Can such faith save him?*

If someone says they are believing God for their healing, yet they spend their days planning their funeral, what do we know? They are *not* believing God for healing. They are not in faith. Were they really in faith, their actions would correspond to their beliefs; they would plan their vacation instead of their funeral. If a person says they are believing God for a new luxury car, yet they make no effort to care for their present vehicle or clean their garage, we know they're not really in faith. Many say they're in faith when they're really just dreaming, wishing, hoping, talking, etc. When a person is in faith, corresponding actions will accompany their words.

FAITH OBEYS

The movement of faith is not random movement; it must be in accordance with God's Word and the Spirit's leading. When God gives instructions, they must be followed explicitly. There were bodies of water that were more convenient for the blind man than the pool of Siloam, but since Jesus told him to go there, he had to go there. The Jordan was not Namaan the Syrian's preferred river, but since the prophet sent him there, he had to wash in *that* river. Those who feel free to modify the Lord's instructions – changing them to suit their own desires – will find themselves lacking the best part of faith: results.

God doesn't tell us everything at once. He gives us partial information: just enough to act upon. Were He to tell us everything up front, faith wouldn't be required and He wouldn't be able to act. When the Apostle Paul, at his conversion, asked God what he should do, God responded, *Go into the city and it shall be told you.* Faith is simple: *Do this. Say that. Go here.* God gave Paul the next step of His plan. Because Paul obeyed that step, going into the city, the next part of His plan for him was revealed.

God has told many people to *Go into the city,* but to them, that's not enough information. They won't go until they know every last detail. Although they say they are believing God for direction, they're really not. They're in disobedience. No matter how much they feed upon or confess the Word, they won't get results until they obey what God told them. They must make the required movement to go along with their faith. They must stop asking questions and just go into the city.

We must train ourselves to instantly obey God's voice. Obedience is no small thing; it can mean life or death for ourselves or someone else. If a person is in the habit of mentally arguing with God's instructions, they will cease hearing His instructions. They will go without God's precious direction and leading and will suffer much defeat and disappointment in life.

I, like others, have had to train myself to obey God's voice. We train ourselves in this area by always obeying the written Word of God. Then, we obey the promptings and leadings of the Holy Spirit. The Word is first. If a person won't obey God's written Word, acting upon it as required, they will never obey a Word given by the Spirit.

When God, several years ago, spoke those three words to me, *Get to Tulsa*, that was the end of our conversation. As I said, I didn't want to move there, but my desires didn't factor into our decision to obey. I had trained myself to obey His voice, regardless of personal preference. I didn't clutter up the decision by asking, *Why Tulsa?* I didn't ask, *What do you want me to do there?* I could sense that He wanted me to go into the city as quickly as possible, so I just focused on getting to the place He assigned me. Within six weeks, I was living in Tulsa.

The movement of faith is not difficult. God has never asked me to do something that was hard or complicated. (It might have been hard on my flesh and mind, but the actions themselves were not hard.) He's never told me to go on an extended fast and He probably never will (He's likely not telling you to go on an extended fast either). People think that if their actions are extreme it will somehow get God's attention and prove their faith. No sir. No ma'am. Extreme actions are rooted in fear rather than faith, the believer scrambling to do something wild as a last-ditch effort to get an answer. I can tell them their answer right now. They need to go back to step one: *faith comes by hearing*. The hearing of faith precedes the movement of faith.

One extreme action that people often take is throwing away their medication. Please hear me carefully: you don't have to throw out your medicine in order to prove that you're in faith. You can take medicine and still be in faith. If you feel as though your faith has brought you to the place where you no longer need your medications, your doctor will confirm that, and he or she can help you safely come off of them. (I have had several church members over the years take themselves off their medications. Not once was it the right decision. I always counsel people to consult with their doctor first.)

There are plenty of actions that are appropriate for the person who is in faith. If you're believing God for a spouse, begin preparing yourself for that spouse. Take the action of keeping your body in good shape so you'll be attractive to your future spouse. Eliminate as much debt from your life as possible so you don't financially encumber a new spouse. These kinds of actions, although not always exciting or extreme, correspond to faith and don't require any special leading.

A WOMAN OF FAITH

And there was a woman who had had a discharge of blood for twelve years, and who had suffered much under many physicians, and had spent all that she had, and was no better but rather grew worse. She had heard the reports about Jesus and came up behind him in the crowd and touched his garment. For she said, "If I touch

*even his garments, I will be made well." And immediate-
ly the flow of blood dried up, and she felt in her body that
she was healed of her disease.*

Mark 5:25-28

This woman had an illness that had ravaged her body for twelve long years and drained her of her finances. Thank God, she was completely healed. Notice, however, what enabled God's healing power to flow to her. First, she heard about Jesus. What did she hear? She must have heard that people everywhere were being healed as they touched Him.

After faith came, she voiced her beliefs, putting her faith into action through words. She said, *If I touch even his garments, I will be made well.* Those words of faith were words that God could inhabit. Faith came. Faith spoke. But that's not all that happened. Had she remained where she was, in the comfort of her living quarters, this story would not have ended as it did; we wouldn't be reading about it these many years later. This woman refused to allow fear to keep her still or hold her back. She arose, making movement that corresponded with her beliefs.

Imagine how weak and frail she must have been after twelve years of constant bleeding. Imagine the thoughts that came against her as she made her way toward the crowd: *You can't do this. Your immune system is compromised. You'll die out there.* She had to overcome her thoughts and the voice of her physical symptoms to begin making movement. The heat, the smell, the crowd. She had to press through it all, but that's what faith does.

It moves when everything in the natural says *stay put*. It runs toward the opposition. It swims upstream and ignores the mainstream. How did all this work out for her? She was set free from a dozen years of disease.

I've had God deal with me at times to begin to make movement towards certain things that He had for me. He has made statements to us such as, *That's your house.* I had to receive the Word I heard from Him, meditating on it until faith came. Then, I spoke words that agreed with His words. Next, I had to make movement toward the particular home He showed me (I couldn't substitute another home that was cheaper or easier on my faith). I set out to make movement without any of the resources to complete the transaction. The resources always came after I stepped out and began to move.

God inhabits the action of our faith with His power. We need not do anything extreme, but must simply take a step in the direction of our faith. God will direct our movement as we look to Him. The actions are as simple as *fill the pots with water*, but the results are miraculous: water being turned into wine. We must be as simple-minded and open-hearted as the servants at the wedding of Cana. Mary told them, *Do whatever He tells you* (John 2:5).

I have a dear friend in ministry who, several years ago, pioneered a new church. They began meeting in a building where they had to set up and tear down their equipment each week. Being a new church, they had to believe for everything, including all their help. In particular, they needed help in the area of music. They released their faith for a keyboard player to come, and were speaking in line with their beliefs. However, they took their faith one step further. They put action to their faith by setting up a keyboard. Each week, they set up that keyboard, connected it to the sound system, and then packed it up after the service was over.

Imagine the thoughts that would come against these pastors for taking action that supported their beliefs. *Why are we going to all the trouble to set this up with no one to play it? People are going to think we're crazy.* Faith cares not what people think; faith is occupied with what God thinks. We give action to our faith because faith is not static or idle. It moves. After a good while – setting it up, tearing it down, setting it up, tearing it down – that keyboard player showed up. In fact, an entire worship team was formed. It matters that appropriate movement accompanies our faith.

If you want your mountain to move, you must move. Put action to your believing and speaking. The Word itself will dictate certain actions that must accompany your believing. At other times, God will specifically direct your action. Either way, be sure to add corresponding actions to your faith. Then you will enjoy faith's results. Faith comes. Faith says. *Faith moves.*

Chapter 15

The Spirit of Faith

As a usual thing, no one likes a fight. Faith, however, is not usual. People of faith have an uncanny desire to be in the ring with an opponent, knowing that as the fight goes longer, they grow stronger. There's no backing down with faith, no looking the other way. If a fight is inevitable, faith will set the terms. Faith will finish it.

When the movie *Captain America* was released several years ago, it depicted a scrawny young man, Steve Rodgers, who seemed to be a magnet for trouble. Because of his size (or lack thereof), people thought him an easy target. They soon found out, however, that they had picked the wrong target. Steve took more punches than he threw, but had an endless amount of fight in him. As he stood, facing his opponent, face bloodied, he would say, *I can do this all day*. That's faith. Faith will ignore the natural and speak the Word all day long. Then, the next day, do it all over again.

Faith doesn't know what it's like to lose. It doesn't understand what it means to quit. Faith never gives up, never lays down. It may get knocked down repeatedly, but it gets back up every time. There's a grittiness to faith: a ruggedness that resembles a lasso-wielding cowboy or a sword-slinging swashbuckler (say that several times, as fast as you can). You don't want to mess with faith. Faith will win if it takes forever. Faith is unconquerable. You can't sink it. You can't quench it. You can't kill it. You can't silence it.

> *Since we have the same **spirit of faith** according to what has been written, "I believed, and so I spoke," we also believe, and so we also speak.*
>
> 2 Corinthians 4:13

Faith believes God, considering His words to be settled fact. It talks about impossibilities as though they had already occurred. It tells what God will do before it happens. It pronounces itself healed when it looks anything but. It declares victory at the beginning of the battle, not the end. It sees the need met and *says* the need met before anything in the natural has changed. Religion doesn't understand this kind of believing and speaking, but God loves it. It gives Him the entrance that He needs to move and work in our life.

Faith-talk is often misunderstood and can be mistaken for arrogance. For example, when you hear the news of an impending recession and you declare, *It won't affect me, I'm recession-free,* that sounds a bit strange. People will wonder why you don't share their fear. You're talking like David when he said, *ten thousand may fall at my right hand, but it won't come near me* (Psalm 91:7). You're operating in the same spirit, or flow, of faith as Caleb and Joshua, who ignored the fact that their promised land was giant-infested. They declared, *Let us go up at once and possess it, for we are well able to overcome* (Numbers 13:30). Faith refuses to move from its persuasion that, *If God said it, I can have it. If God said it, it's mine now.*

THROWING BEYOND

> *But we have this treasure in jars of clay, to show that the surpassing power belongs to God and not to us. We are afflicted in every way, but not crushed; perplexed, but not driven to despair; persecuted, but not forsaken; struck down, but not destroyed.*
>
> *2 Corinthians 4:7-9*

In this passage, Paul speaks of God's *surpassing power*: the spiritual power that's available to every believer. The Greek word translated as *surpassing* is interesting, found only a few times in the New Testament (twice in this chapter). It means *a throwing beyond.* The power that indwells us is a power that throws beyond, glory to God! God's power will take us beyond that which is usual or normal. It will take us farther than we thought possible. His power is an exceeding power: exceeding every need.

This power that *throws beyond* seems to work most effectively, not in times of ease or comfort, but in times of pressure and testing. The greater the pressure, the greater the effect of the power. Look again at verses 8-9:

> *We are afflicted in every way, but not crushed; perplexed, but not driven to despair; persecuted, but not forsaken; struck down, but not destroyed.*

Some have the wrong idea that if faith is present, tests and trials will be absent. The opposite is true. Tests and trials aid in the development of faith. As the great man of faith, Smith Wigglesworth, was fond of saying, *There are no victories without battles; no testimonies without tests.* Although the enemy brings difficulties into our life for our destruction, faith will cause those attacks to instead benefit our lives.

Let's take a closer look at each of these four statements by Paul:

We are afflicted in every way, but not crushed

Afflicted in *every way*. That means no area of Paul's life was unaffected. He encountered constant and extreme challenges to the abundant life that God provided. What does it mean to be afflicted? Many think it to be a reference to sickness and disease, but that's not the case. *Afflicted*, in the New Testament, simply means *pressure*. Paul was saying, *We are experiencing pressure in every possible area and in every possible way.*

PRESSURE

When pressure comes, people often think it means their faith isn't working. No, pressure comes because the enemy recognizes that your faith *is* working. He desperately tries to slow and stop the movement of your faith by turning up the heat, manipulating whatever circumstances he can. Faith awakens pressure. (If there's no pressure in your life, that's not a good sign. It may mean there's no faith.) And, pressure awakens faith. When pressure comes, it must be met with faith. More pressure must be met with more faith.

What was the result of the intense pressure that Paul experienced? His defeat? His demise? No. He said that he was *not crushed*.

If I held an empty soda can in my hand and began to apply pressure, that can would quickly be crushed. If, however, the can was made from eighth-inch-thick steel instead of thin aluminum, it could not be crushed by my hand. The thicker material makes the can stronger than the surrounding pressure. (This is why submarines are not made from soda-can-strength aluminum.) Faith lines our life with a layer of spiritual armor. Faith cannot be crushed.

The word translated as *crushed* literally means *brought to a narrow place*. The purpose of the enemy's pressure is to corral our lives into a narrow space. He means to make us smaller, squeezing us so as to reduce our footprint in the Kingdom of God. He works incessantly to force us into smaller spaces. God, on the other hand, is all about enlargement. His Word and the leading of His Spirit work together to bring us into greater places and larger spaces. God wants our lives bigger. The good news? The pressure that comes to make our lives smaller can instead fuel our enlargement.

Growing up in sunny South Florida, I spent most of my youth in the swimming pool. My brother and I had many games we would play in the pool, but one of our favorites was simply to submerge a beach ball. As that ball was held down, the pressure of the water moved against it. When we released the ball, it would shoot up out of the water, into the air. The further down we held the ball, the greater the pressure and the higher the flight. Pressure, often a destructive force, can instead be a propelling force. It's faith that causes the enemy's pressure to propel us instead of destroy us. The greater the pressure, the higher we go.

Perplexed, but not driven to despair.

Perplexed means *to have no way out*. Have you ever been in a situation where there was no apparant way out – no exit? What does a person do when there's no way out? Most give up hope and accept defeat. Not faith. When faith has no way out, it makes a way out. There's *always* a way with faith. Faith always has another card in its hand, another play in the book. Faith puts God – the One who creates something from nothing – in the midst of the equation. God makes a way where there is no way.

I will make a way in the wilderness and rivers in the desert.

Isaiah 43:19

There's never a time when it's right to give up and agree with the impossibility. Just because the answer is not apparent doesn't mean there's no answer. All it means is that the answer isn't in our mind. The answer is in the spirit – the God-realm – and faith will lay hold of it. Although our mental resources may be easily exhausted, our spiritual resources are unlimited. There's no need to despair when Heaven's resources are at our disposal. We must learn to forsake the natural and live in the spirit: the realm of answers, direction, and peace.

Persecuted, but not forsaken.

When we think of persecution, we often think of what Paul went through: government leaders, commoners, and everyone in between rising up against him. Paul experienced persecution on a daily basis. Think about one instance, where a group of forty men vowed not to eat anything until they had killed him. I know how motivated I get when I miss even one meal. These men must have been doing everything possible to kill Paul so they could get back home in time for dinner.

What does faith do when a group of men are trying to kill you? Faith remains steadfast in its belief in God's deliverance and help. How did it turn out for Paul? The town's leading official gave him an escort of five hundred soldiers to transport him safely on his way. Instead of dying at the hands of the *Hunger Strike Clan*, he received an all-expense-paid, first-class ticket to the next place God was sending him. If those forty men were true to their word, I imagine they all died from hunger. They never did kill Paul.

Persecution can be intense, as Paul could easily testify. We, however, know little of that bounty-on-your-head kind of persecution today. Persecution, in the Bible, often just means *opposition*. Opposition can come to us through people (as with Paul), or it can be spiritual: the work of the enemy as he influences circumstances. Either way, there's good news. When we're persecuted (opposed), we're not forsaken.

BEHIND

The word *forsaken* means *to be left behind*. The enemy has badgered me over the years, trying to convince me that God, for some reason, has left me behind. *Look at everyone else. Look at how successful they are. Look at all the ministry opportunities they have. Look at how many people are in their church. Look at how many ministry partners they have. Look at what they live in. Look at what they drive.*

Are these kinds of thoughts familiar to you? We must reject them, keeping our focus where it belongs: on pleasing and serving God. The enemy wants all of us to believe and act like we've been forsaken. He wants us to believe that we've been left behind. Financially, physically, in marriage, at work, the enemy tries to convince you that you'll never catch up; that you'll always be behind. If he can get us to believe that, he can bring it to pass in our life.

God, however, doesn't want us behind. He puts His power in our life for the purpose of undoing the devil's work, advancing us further than we ever thought possible. The devil works to drive us backward, but God's surpassing power throws us beyond. *From behind to beyond.* That's God's plan. Any step back is simply the windup to throw you forward. This is what God's surpassing power will do, but it only works when faith is present and active. God's power, working by faith, takes us from behind to beyond.

How did Paul respond to the pressure that seemed to be pushing him back? He answered it with faith-filled words. He spoke, focusing not on the pressure but on God's power. The pressure that came to make him smaller instead fueled his enlargement. The circumstances that came to crush him instead propelled him. Instead of getting smaller, he got bigger. More cities were reached, more churches established, more people saved. He went from behind to beyond.

Struck down, but not destroyed.

When Paul spoke of the pressure that he was experiencing, he followed each statement with the word *but.* We are afflicted, *but.* We are opposed, *but.* We are perplexed, *but.* The last statement he made was *struck down, but not destroyed. Destroyed* means *brought to an end.* That's one of the enemy's favorite lies: *You've reached the end. There's no way out this time.* Friends, when it looks like you've reached the end and your back is up against the wall, faith will use the wall as a launching pad to spring you out.

When circumstances say, *There's no way*, learn, like Paul, to declare, *But. Yes, it looks bad, BUT God is greater*.

Many use that word *but* in times of difficulty, but they use it to speak words of doubt and unbelief. They say, *I know the Word says I'm healed, but the doctors say this can't be treated. I know the Word says God supplies all my needs, but the bills are really stacking up. I know God called me to this church, but I just don't think the pastor appreciates me*. That's not the right way to use this word *but*. I often tell people they need to get their *but* in the right place. If you're speaking words of doubt and unbelief, move your *but*. Speak words of faith. This is how Paul received deliverance from every test and trial.

Notice just a few more verses from this chapter:

> *For our momentary light burden of affliction is working out for us more and more surpassingly an eternal, heavy weight of glory while we are not contemplating the things that are seen but the things which are not seen, for the things which are seen are temporary, but the things which are not seen are eternal.*
>
> *2 Corinthians 4:17-18 (WST)*

Any circumstance in your life – *anything* in this natural realm – is temporary: subject to change. I'll say it again: if it's in your life, it can change. Don't let anyone, no matter how well-meaning, well-educated, or well-respected, tell you that a situation in your life can't turn around. Don't listen to anyone who tells you to just give up and accept your present circumstances as your *lot in life*. Well-meaning preachers may encourage you to settle, conform, and adapt. Nonsense. Don't adapt. Advance! Christians who don't know any better will tell you it's holy and godly to back down and embrace life's limitations. That's not holy, it's compromise. It's faithless. Never settle for less when God offers you His best.

Don't allow the circumstances of life to dictate your believing, saying, and moving. Don't believe that things will always be the way they are today. There's a way out, and it's faith. Faith changes that which looks unchangeable. It imposes the eternal upon the temporal. It reverses that which appears irreversible. It makes the impossible possible.

I love verse 17 in this passage:

> *For our momentary light burden of affliction is working out for us more and more surpassingly an eternal, heavy weight of glory.*

We've already spoken of some of the opposition that Paul faced. I'm reminded of another instance, when the leaders of Damascus wanted to kill him. In order to escape death, Paul's fellow believers lowered him down the wall of the city in a basket. In case this sounds like fun, be assured it was not. Baskets are not the most stable form of transportation. It was nighttime, and the walls of Damascus were more than just a few feet high. This was likely a terrifying experience but, when faced with death and the elevators aren't working, faith jumps into a basket. Faith moves.

Being lowered in a basket was easy compared to some of the other circumstances Paul endured. He was whipped and beaten multiple times and survived shipwrecks in waters with who-knows-what swimming underneath. We could go on and on, concluding that Paul had a rough life (although he would disagree). The point is, when he said he had *pressure on every side*, he meant it. That's why his statement in verse 17 is so amazing.

He called his problems a *momentary light burden of affliction*. Light pressure. Really? Was Paul just putting on an air of spirituality or did he really consider all that he was going through to be light? Think back to our illustration of the aluminum can versus a steel cylinder. If I used the pressure of my hand to squeeze the aluminum can, it would quickly give way. If, however, I squeezed the steel cylinder, nothing would happen. That steel cylinder, were it able to feel, would barely feel the pressure of my hand.

Paul's spirit was strengthened through his daily intake of God's Word. He barely felt problems that would crush most believers. Our spirit can become similarly strong. (If we are to be victorious in life's battles, our spirit *must* become strong.) Imagine how it frustrates the enemy when he hits you with his knockout blow and you look around and say, *I thought I felt something, but I guess it was nothing*.

It's possible to grow to the place where pressure is coming against you from every direction and you barely notice. Like Paul, you'll consider your troubles light and temporary. Perspective is everything with faith. We must develop until we see God as big as He is and our problems as small as they are. There's a saying in the world: *Don't sweat the small stuff.* That statement is usually followed by this one: *Everything is small stuff.* Faith sees the enemy's biggest attacks as small, light, and temporary.

The story is told of Smith Wigglesworth who, one night, was awakened as he sensed an evil presence in his room. There, sitting on the edge of his bed, was Satan himself, in physically manifested form. How would you react in such a situation? Brother Smith looked over at him, said, *Oh, it's just you,* and then rolled over to go back to sleep. May we come to share Brother Wigglesworth's perspective. May we learn to see the devil – the god of this world – as insignificant as he really is.

PLEASURE IN PRESSURE

Paul considered his problems light because he considered God heavy. He saw his problems small because he saw God big. Notice verse 17 again, this time in the *New King James Version*:

> *For our light affliction, which is but for a moment, is* **working for us** *a far more exceeding and eternal weight of glory.*

The pressure that's coming against you is really working for you. What revelation! This explains why Jesus, after telling us we would have problems in this world (John 16:33), commanded us to be happy. This is why Paul said he took pleasure in pressure (2 Corinthians 12:10). The moment trouble shows up, the dev-

149

il will be right there, telling you that destruction is imminent. God, however, tells us that the things that are working against us are actually working for us. That's happy news indeed. New problems? That's fine. They can join my workforce, helping to propel my life beyond.

The enemy brings pressure in order to push us backward in life. We must respond to that pressure with faith. When we do, it's like backing up one of those spring-loaded toy cars. Although the car is momentarily moving backwards, its release propels it forward with a power that ordinarily wouldn't be present. Faith spring-loads our life, causing backward pressure to fuel our forward thrust.

Don't be discouraged by difficulties or delay. Don't view reverse movement as defeat. Let the pressure wind the springs of your life in order to throw you beyond. It's the backward motion of a catapult that sends the object soaring forward. The backward movement of a slingshot sends the stone through the air. The retracting of the bow sends the arrow speeding ahead. Does it look like you're going backward? Praise God! You're on your launching pad. Lean back and get ready to fly.

Chapter 16

Faith Wins

The final point to the sermon the Lord gave me that night before bed was *Faith wins*. I easily understood the first three points but initially lacked clarity on this fourth point; it wasn't until I began to teach this message that I began to see more clearly. I had thought that *faith wins* was simply the result of performing the other three steps (faith comes + faith says + faith moves = faith wins). The Lord helped me see, however, that *faith wins* is more than just the result of hearing, saying, and doing. The winning of faith is its own step: an essential but seldom practiced part of the process of faith.

How does a sports team act when they have the game in hand – they know they've won – and there's not enough time for their opponent to mount a comeback? They start rejoicing in their victory, even before the clock has run out. Winning is an exuberant, joy-filled event. The winning of faith is likewise joy-filled. Rejoicing is how faith wins. We don't wait until the end of the game to begin rejoicing; we start out rejoicing. Faith wins while it looks like it's still losing.

It's this last step of faith that is in some ways the most powerful, for it's the step that brings the manifestation of the answer into the natural realm. It's also an often-neglected step, for it makes little sense to the natural mind. Who rejoices when fighting a life-or-death battle? Faith does. Who rejoices when facing bankruptcy? Faith does. Who rejoices when severe symptoms arise? Faith does. No matter the challenge, faith rejoices. Faith wins.

Why does faith rejoice? Because faith sees the need as having already been met. It sees the answer as having already been received. It sees the body as having already been healed. Since people of faith believe they receive when they pray (Mark 11:24), the natural expressions that follow are expressions of gladness and joy. Rejoicing that the answer has been received is the activity that occurs between releasing faith into action, and the point where the answer manifests in the natural realm.

People often ask if there's anything they can do to speed up the process of faith: to experience the manifestation of their answer more quickly. There sure is, and it's this step. You can rejoice. You can praise. You can give thanks. You can shout and dance. You can laugh. You can win. A constant flow of rejoicing will cause your answer to show up faster. Many stall, delay, and even cancel out their faith by living in the realm of feelings and reason, identifying with the problem and talking about the problem. They walk by sight instead of faith.

REJOICING ALWAYS

> *Be rejoicing in the Lord* **always**. *Again I say, Be rejoic-ing.*
>
> Philippians 4:4 (WST)

Always. We must ask ourselves how well we are obeying this verse. Did the writer really mean *always*? If he didn't, we're in trouble. If one verse in the Bible is unreliable, every other part can be called into question. Thank God, we know that every word of Scripture is accurate: included on purpose. There are no exaggerations or speaking off the top of one's head. Paul told us to be *rejoicing always*. To do anything else is to live in disobedi-ence. If he said *always*, he meant *always*.

Always means *at all times*. We could say it this way: *in every situation and on every occasion*. We understand that it's not phys-ically possible to perform any activity 24 hours a day. *Always* simply means it's your constant practice – your regular occupa-tion – your habit.

Many are confused as to how to properly practice this verse, or even whether to practice it. They think, *That's unrealistic. I'm not happy all the time. Sometimes I'm sad and down.* I under-stand that feelings change from moment to moment but faith doesn't. To go around discouraged and depressed is to live in un-belief. Many teach that yielding to discouragement is acceptable, but according to Scripture, it's not. *But you don't understand how hard I've had it.* Yes, and you don't understand faith.

Maybe you haven't had the most pleasant life, but it's doubtful that you've experienced even a fraction of what others have experienced. Here's yet another example from the life of the Apostle Paul.

Paul was a prisoner aboard a ship, held against his will for the crime of preaching the gospel. That ship encountered a terrible storm that lasted for weeks. Can you imagine being tossed up and down in the raging sea for three solid weeks? Can you imagine how many times he and the rest of the passengers got sick? After a while, they just stopped eating; I'm sure everything they ate came right back up. The Bible says they didn't eat for a period of 14 days.

The sailors finally ran the ship aground where it was broken apart by violent waves. Anyone who wanted to live had to grab a piece of the boat and paddle ashore. They made it to shore, soaked and shivering, when some wise-guy uttered the proverbial comment, *It could be worse. It could be raining.* As if on cue, the heavens opened, pouring down rain. They began to freeze all over again. Not until they meet some of the locals do they realize that the island is inhabited by barbarians. If the storm at sea didn't kill them, perhaps their new neighbors would.

The idea is presented to build a large fire, to which all agree. Paul, not one to sit idly by, does his part, gathering sticks to burn. As he reaches down for a handful of branches, out comes a poisonous viper, attaching himself to Paul's hand. He has maybe ten or fifteen minutes to live. May I ask, how's your day, in comparison?

This wasn't Paul's worst month, by the way. It was actually more or less typical for him. One might think that after all these difficulties he would be like Eeyore from *Winnie the Pooh*, the gentle but gloom-filled donkey who spread depression everywhere he went. *Poor ole' me* was Eeyore's mantra. Paul wouldn't be caught dead uttering such unbelieving words or hanging his head in despair. Paul was a person of faith, through and through. He heard, spoke, moved, and won.

Paul didn't die from that snake bite, incidentally. He shook the snake off and was supernaturally spared death. The testimony of his miraculous healing caused the whole island to turn to the Lord. Revival broke out because he chose faith over unbelief and rejoicing over despair. Think of what would happen in our churches and communities if God's people today chose to get serious about rejoicing. We'd get results like Paul. Although still classified as a prisoner, his situation improved dramatically. When it came time for him to resume traveling, the leader of the island sent him on his way to Rome aboard a luxury cruiser.

This same Paul, who endured unthinkable and continued hardship, is the one who emphatically issued the command, *Rejoice in the Lord always*. We must ask, did Paul practice what he preached? Did he rejoice in the midst of the mess he was in? We know he did. On that ship, when the situation looked darkest, Paul told everyone to get happy. He had heard from God that they would all make it to safety (Acts 27:22). Since Paul rejoiced always, we know that on the ship, in the water, on shore in the rain, and with a deadly viper hanging off his wrist, Paul rejoiced. Had he not, he would have no right to expect the same of us.

Why rejoice when you have only minutes to live? How could anyone feel happy and joyful in such devastating trouble? Here's what many fail to understand: Paul *didn't* feel happy and joyful in these circumstances. The Bible never mentions Paul feeling an ounce of joy, nor does it ever tell us to *feel* joyful. In the natural, the act of rejoicing must be preceded by feelings of joy, but in the Kingdom of God, the two can be unrelated. One may rejoice without any joyful feelings whatsoever. With faith, feelings are irrelevant.

Bible rejoicing is an act, not a feeling. The requirement that we rejoice means we express joy, irrespective of feelings. We can begin to rejoice while feeling depressed. As we obey and begin to express joy by faith, our expressions of joy will eventually usher in feelings of joy. The act of rejoicing sends depression packing and turns frowns to smiles. We express joy based on the truth in God's Word rather than the present facts in this world.

What are these expressions of joy with which the believer must be occupied? The same expressions we are familiar with in the natural realm: laughing, dancing, shouting, jumping, twirling, etc. The first and most common of these expressions is laughter.

*When the Lord restored the fortunes of Zion, we were like those who dream. Then **our mouth was filled with laughter, and our tongue with shouts of joy;** then they* *said among the nations, "The Lord has done great things for them."*

Psalms 126:1-2

Most people laugh when things are light-hearted and funny. Faith, however, laughs when things are life-threatening and serious. Faith-laughter has a different tone than natural laughter, as it is not inspired by joyful feelings. Faith-laughter, inspired only by the truth of God's Word, is often expressed in the face of fear and impending doom. Faith's laughter might start out slow and dry: *Ha, ha, ha.*

As the believer continues to rejoice by faith, the Spirit of God will come upon him or her, causing their expressions of joy to be filled with divine joy. The rejoicing that started out purely by faith now has corresponding feelings attached. This rejoicing is powerful, as it lays hold of the object of desire and pulls it into the natural realm. Faith becomes sight as joy prevails. Answers manifest during the winning phase of faith.

I love the testimony that Rev. Kenneth E. Hagin shares along these lines. One evening, while on the road ministering, he was awakened with severe heart symptoms. Could any situation be more dire? Would there ever be a better time to skip faith and just head for the hospital? That depends if you want to live or die. For some, who have no available supply of faith, they had better get to the hospital right away. In Brother Hagin's case, there was no time for a hospital. He needed his faith right then. Thankfully, his habit of feeding on God's Word made a supply of spiritual strength available.

Brother Hagin pulled the covers up over his head, so as not to disturb the pastor sleeping in the next room, and began to laugh out loud: *Ha, ha, ha.* He repeated this over and over. There was nothing inspired about his laughter at all; not even the slightest feeling of joy (who feels joyful when dying?) He continued to laugh until his victory manifested. Every symptom left and he was perfectly well. This didn't happen in one or two minutes. He had to persist, laughing without inspiration or feelings, until he was well.

His laughter was not in place of the other steps of faith, but came alongside those steps. In this case, laughing was both the moving and winning phase. While he was laughing, the truth arose within him that Jesus had already provided his healing for him. There was nothing left for Brother Hagin to do but receive and rejoice. Those two words are connected: rejoicing and receiving. There's no receiving without rejoicing. There's no manifestation without praising.

PURE JOY

> *Consider it a matter for unadulterated joy [without any admixture of sorrow] whenever you fall into the midst of variegated trials which surround you.*
>
> James 1:2 (WST)

This verse in James is specific: 100% pure joy with no tones of sorrow, defeat, or doubt.

Anyone can rejoice when things look good, but this verse specifies full joy when surrounded by trials of every kind. When things look as though they couldn't be worse, we must rejoice as though they couldn't be better. To be clear: this is not optional. You must do this, and must continue to do this for as long as necessary. There's no winning the battle without the winning of faith. If you want your answer to show up, you'll have to rejoice your way there.

> *We can rejoice, too, when we run into problems and trials, for we know that they help us develop endurance. And endurance develops strength of character, and character strengthens our confident hope of salvation. And this hope will not lead to disappointment. For we know how dearly God loves us, because he has given us the Holy Spirit to fill our hearts with his love.*
>
> *Romans 5:3-5 (NLT)*

This passage teaches that if we will respond with joy as we face problems and trials, we will not be disappointed with the outcome. The result will be consistent with God's loving nature: we will receive our answer.

We must meet the trial of our faith with joy. Notice, this passage specifies rejoicing *when we run into problems*. This is speaking of our initial contact: when we first learn about the situation. Our first response to a test or trial should be a rousing round of rejoicing. (I don't know about you, but my natural reaction to trouble has *never* been joy.) I've had to train myself in this area, living full enough of God's Word and Spirit to respond appropriately to life's difficulties. Although feelings might dictate a different response, we must respond with joy. We must begin rejoicing when we feel like crying.

We meet our problems with joy, rejoice in the midst of our problems, and continue in joy all the way to the end of the problem. Why such an emphasis on rejoicing and praising? It's the only thing that works. It's a necessary part of our daily life; a necessary part of faith. Along with hearing, saying, and moving, the rejoicing of faith must be continually present. The believer – any believer – can rejoice his or her way out of anything and rejoice his or her way into anything.

> *Whom having not seen, ye love; in whom, though now ye see him not, yet believing, ye rejoice with joy unspeakable and full of glory: Receiving the end of your faith, even the salvation of your souls.*
>
> *1 Peter 1:8-9 (KJV)*

Rejoicing takes us to *the end of our faith*. The end of our faith is the goal of our faith: the place where that which previously looked impossible has come to pass. Every believer wants to arrive at faith's finish line, but we can't reach the finish line without faith-filled expressions of joy. We must praise, run, dance, laugh, and shout our way to the finish line, without any supporting evidence in the natural. Anyone can rejoice when their answer manifests but faith rejoices ahead of time. We continue these expressions of joy until the answer appears in the natural realm. We rejoice until our faith becomes sight.

The Bible provides a clear path to victory for the believer who is facing tests and trials. That path emphasizes one action above all others: rejoicing. That's the last thing anyone would think of when facing a heavy test or trial, but it's exactly what must happen. There is no alternative. Crying, counseling, analyzing, worrying: none of these can substitute for rejoicing. I'll say it again: the *one thing* that the Bible emphasizes above all else when in a test or trial is rejoicing. You can laugh, dance, and shout your problems away.

We don't just rejoice in times of difficulty; we are to rejoice *always*: at all times. Faith isn't just for the hard places, it's also for the good things that we are believing for: things that are not seen and not yet. We must rejoice about these things as well, continuing until the unseen becomes seen. Rejoice about the things you're believing for. Don't wait until the item shows up. Rejoice now. Faith is now.

Many would like new homes or cars. God may even have directed you toward one. You may have heard, prayed, and begun to move, but now what? Now you win. You rejoice from the time you say *Amen* until the item is in your name.

While you're in your current home, see yourself in your new home. By faith, dance in your new kitchen. Do this every day: every time you think of it. While you're driving around in your current car, praise God for the new one that you've already received. By faith, drive that new car, thanking God for how nice it is and how strong it runs. Don't mindlessly listen to the radio. Turn that off and turn on your praise. Let your own songs come forth from your spirit. Most believers won't do this. They choose to live spiritually dry. That's why they don't get to the end of their faith. That's why they don't win.

The Body of Christ has fallen behind in this area of rejoicing, praise, worship, and thanksgiving. That's why we hear so few testimonies of faith. Elements such as prayer are important, but praying can't take the place of rejoicing. Even in our prayer services, much time should be given to faith-filled expressions of joy, praise, and thanks. It's these expressions that bring the manifestation of our faith to the forefront. People fail to win with their faith because they leave off the winning phase of faith. Don't stop rejoicing. Don't stop praising. Don't stop winning. *Faith wins.*

Chapter 17

Faith Like Abraham

My favorite Bible passage on the subject of faith is found in Romans chapter four. It chronicles the account of Abraham and his wife, Sarah, as they held fast to God's promise of a son. Sarah, you may recall, had been barren her whole life. Now ninety years old, she was that much more incapable of childbirth. Abraham had fathered children, but was now almost one hundred years old: way too late for kids. To think that Abraham and Sarah could together conceive a child after decades of failed attempts was beyond absurd, yet, God promised Abraham and Sarah just that. They were to have a son of their own.

Let's read this great passage:

> *That is why it depends on faith, in order that the promise may rest on grace and be guaranteed to all his offspring—not only to the adherent of the law but also to*

the one who shares the faith of Abraham, who is the father of us all, as it is written, "I have made you the father of many nations"—in the presence of the God in whom he believed, who gives life to the dead and calls into existence the things that do not exist. In hope he believed against hope, that he should become the father of many nations, as he had been told, "So shall your offspring be." He did not weaken in faith when he considered his own body, which was as good as dead (since he was about a hundred years old), or when he considered the barrenness of Sarah's womb. No unbelief made him waver concerning the promise of God, but he grew strong in his faith as he gave glory to God, fully convinced that God was able to do what he had promised.

Romans 4:16-21

Abraham went wherever God told him and did whatever God said. He heard, spoke, and moved in agreement with God's plan. In return, God gave him vast resources, a long healthy life, tremendous honor and influence, and a heritage to carry on his legacy of faith. God gave these things to Abraham by His grace, but Abraham had to receive them by faith. He had to hear, say, move, and rejoice in agreement with God.

We are encouraged by multiple New Testament authors to look to Abraham as our example of what a person of faith can possess, accomplish, and become. We can have what Abraham had if we'll do what Abraham did. This passage teaches us how he received. Notice the very first phrase: *it depends on faith.*

Faith, as we have stated, is not an option if one is to receive from God. We sometimes hear people talk about the *faith message* or a *faith church* as though the faith-life were one of many available options for the believer. No, a church that's not a faith church is a false church. A message that doesn't include faith is not the gospel. There's no such thing as a genuine church where no one receives from God. The faith of the believer is the determining factor in their receiving. Our receiving *depends on faith.*

When faith is present and active, God's promises are *guaranteed to all his offspring.* To say something is guaranteed means there's no chance of failure; the recipient of the promise can be assured of the outcome. The promises God has given His children are fully guaranteed. They work for all, not just a few. When God told Abraham he and Sarah would have a son, that promise was guaranteed. As long as Abraham brought his faith, there was no chance that the promise would fail to come to pass. In the natural, the opposite looked true. It looked like there was no chance that it *would* come to pass.

Verse 18 shows us the process of faith in action:

> *In hope he believed against hope, that he should become the father of many nations, as he had been told, "So shall your offspring be."*

Remember, we said *hope* means *expectation.* Abraham *believed against hope,* meaning that when there was no reason in the natural for him to expect a child, he and Sarah expected any-way. That's faith. Faith confidently expects the answer to show up, even when no natural evidence supports that expectation.

Notice, in particular, the word *against*. We use our faith against things: against pressure, against lack, against sickness, against opposition. Abraham used his faith against the physical impossi-bility of childbirth. Faith, when up against an impossibility, will remove that impossibility, clearing the way for God's power to flow. Like Abraham, we must use our faith against mountains of impossibility that we may face.

We need not wait for some major issue to arise to begin using our faith. God will continually put projects on our heart to help stretch our faith. For example, He may say, *Give an extra $500 to your church.* We might think God would only say that when we have an extra $500 laying around, but that's not the case. He will often lead us to do that which our resources deem unwise or impossible.

How do you give $500 that you don't have? Step one: *faith comes.* What did God say in His Word and what has He told you by His Spirit? Find out what He has said about provision and meditate upon it until it explodes within you. Then – only then – has faith come. Once faith has come, *faith says.* Claim that $500 from this world's system. Charge the angels to bring in the money and believe you receive when you pray or say. Next, *faith moves.* Make movement that corresponds with your be-liefs. Write a check for $500 and place it where you can easily see it (but don't give it yet, of course). Start setting aside money as it comes in. Lastly, *faith wins*. Rejoice and praise God that you presently have that $500 to give. Continue rejoicing until the money is in the bank and the check is in the offering.

In our illustration above, you used your faith *against* the lack or deficiency that told you that giving your church $500 was unrealistic. Now that you've believed God for $500, pay attention to the leading of His Spirit. He will likely lead you to stretch and grow your faith further by prompting you to give even more. As you use your faith against impossibilities – even small impossibilities like $500 – your faith will grow.

If you sat me down at a bench press machine, loaded it with all the weights, and told me to move it, I can tell you what will happen. Nothing. It wouldn't move. I would press all my strength against that machine to no avail. I would need you to remove most of the weight and then let me try again. As I continued to use my strength against those weights, at a level I could handle, my strength would increase and I would be able to handle more. The more my strength grew and developed, the more weight I could handle.

That's a picture of faith. Faith is spiritual muscle. Only when we use our faith against situations in the natural does it grow and develop. Faith comes by hearing, but it doesn't grow and develop without being used (exercised). Like natural muscle, faith is built through repetition and resistance. There's nothing random or accidental about faith's development. Many believers take no thought for the development of their faith. That's why, when attempting to use faith, they just bounce off their mountains instead of moving them.

When you push with your faith and nothing happens, don't blame the mountain. Don't blame the preacher. Don't blame the Word. Don't blame God. Don't blame faith. There's nothing wrong with faith. It works just fine. You just need to take off some of the weight. Break the problem down into smaller parts that your faith can handle. Begin to move those smaller parts one at a time and your faith will grow.

Verse 19 in this passage is amazing:

> *He did not weaken in faith when he considered his own body, which was as good as dead (since he was about a hundred years old), or when he considered the barrenness of Sarah's womb.*

Abraham was obviously aware of his age and the current reproductive status of both he and his wife. This verse tells us that he faced those natural facts, yet chose to discount them, embracing God's Word instead. This is tremendous. When you're able to look natural circumstances in the face and say, *I see you, I recognize you, but I choose not to give an ounce of credence to you,* you're in faith. Abraham was far more convinced of the veracity of God's Word than he was of natural circumstance. He understood that circumstances, no matter how well aligned with natural law, are still temporary and subject to change. God's Word, on the other hand, cannot change.

WAVERING

Many focus on the circumstances they encounter, allowing those circumstances to weaken their faith. When we give attention to the natural at the expense of God's Word, our faith will be compromised. I understand that the natural must be tended to in some measure, but when we allow the impossibility of the situation to occupy our mind, our spirit will be weakened. We must face what we're dealing with, sure, but then make every effort to replace the natural facts with God's truth. Those who focus on the natural will end up tossed back and forth, becoming what James called *double-minded*. The double-minded person cannot receive from God.

> *But let him ask in faith, nothing wavering. For he that wavereth is like a wave of the sea driven with the wind and tossed. For let not that man think that he shall receive any thing of the Lord. A double minded man is unstable in all his ways.*
>
> James 1:6-8 (KJV)

Double-mindedness is also referred to in this passage as *wavering*. Wavering occurs when a person fluctuates between their beliefs and natural circumstance. When that person is in a good church service, their faith is strengthened and they are encouraged. As soon as they are away from the Word, however, facing natural evidence, they move off their beliefs and begin to take sides with the natural. They are double-minded and will soon become double-tongued, speaking about the problem more than the answer. The back-and-forth of wavering stalls the process of faith.

The next verse in our passage in Romans 4 also speaks of wavering.

> *No unbelief made him waver concerning the promise of God, but he grew strong in his faith as he gave glory to God.*
>
> *Romans 4:20*

Circumstances are not only strong and persistent, they can be constant. Physical pain, for example, can be continually present in one's body; a constant reminder of the reality of the problem. Although the Word of God declares that Jesus carried our pain (Matthew 8:17), the presence of pain will contest that truth. The believer, going through such a trial, will be tempted to waver. The pain in their body will continually speak to them: *I'm real. Feel me. Believe in me. Give in to me.* That ongoing voice can only be quenched by a continual flow of God's Word.

Abraham's 100-year-old body, although healthy, talked to him constantly. It said, *No child is coming from you, old man.* Every time he looked at his 90-year-old wife, moving slower this year than last, the voice of natural circumstances said, *No child is coming out of her, either.* The voice of the natural would have been easy to believe. No child had *ever* come out of Sarah. What did Abraham do with all this natural evidence? He discounted every bit of it. He rejected it, replacing it with the truth of God's Word. He understood that the natural means nothing next to the eternal, unchanging Word of God.

We're told that *no unbelief made him waver.* No unbelief. That's a phrase I would like God to be able to use to describe me. How does a person get to the place where he or she has no unbelief? Unbelief is eradicated only when replaced with faith. Faith must come, rising to levels that exceed evidence in the natural. Then, faith must be maintained over time by continued hearing. Abraham was so settled regarding God's character, ability, and promises, that he considered God's Word to be an established fact. There was no room for argument or reasoning. There was no wavering, no double-mindedness. If God said it was so, it was so. We, like Abraham, must rid our lives of unbelief.

The last part of this verse says *he grew strong in his faith as he gave glory to God.*

There are two acceptable interpretations of this verse. First, it could be said that Abraham gave glory to God in the sense that his life of faith glorified and drew attention to God. That would certainly be true. But, we also know that Abraham gave glory to God in the sense of offering praise to God. Rejoicing (along with worship, praise, and thanksgiving) is a necessary and ongoing part of the process of faith. It's the winning stage of faith, the part that draws in the answer.

The more Abraham rejoiced and praised God, the stronger he became in his convictions. As he praised, he would remind himself that God, for decades, had already proven Himself faithful. As he thought about his long-awaited son, excitement and expectation bubbled up within. Believing that this was already an accomplished fact, Abraham offered expressions of joy and praise as though the baby were already in the crib.

Here's the last verse in this great passage:

> *Fully convinced that God was able to do what he had promised.*
>
> *Romans 4:21*

Abraham so immersed himself in God's promise that he grew to the place where nothing could persuade him otherwise. He was *fully convinced*. To Abraham, Isaac was a reality long before he was born. Abraham's reception of God's promise enabled the conception of a child. The couple's spiritual expectation caused them to be *expecting* in pregnancy. Faith brought Isaac into the world. Faith gives birth to things.

Believers who immerse themselves in the promises of God will, like Abraham, arrive at a place of fully persuaded faith. They *know* God is faithful to His Word. They *know* that what He has said will change any circumstance in the natural. They *know* that it's impossible for God to lie. They're not wondering if faith might work, they know it works; they practice faith every single day. They live by faith, walk by faith, speak words of faith, and rule and reign by faith. They have faith like Abraham.

Abraham's blessing is ours. Redemption's benefits are available. Mountains can be removed; answers are guaranteed. God stands ready to release His mighty power, bringing to pass your full deliverance. He delights to fulfill your dreams and desires. He awaits one thing: faith. The believer has the responsibility of receiving all God has given. Receiving from God isn't difficult, it's simple: *Faith comes, Faith says, Faith moves, Faith wins!*

Salvation

The most important decision you can make in life is the decision to receive Jesus Christ as your personal Lord and Savior. It is a decision to turn from sin and self, and to follow God, every day and in every way.

This decision to receive Christ is what the Bible calls being *born again*, or being *saved*. Without this salvation experience, people are doomed to failure in life and eternity in hell. Success and eternal life belong to the believer in Christ. If you have been reading this book and don't know that you have been born-again, it's time to make the decision to follow Christ.

Read what God says in His word about this great experience:

Truly, truly, I say to you, whoever hears my word and believes him who sent me has eternal life. He does not come into judgment, but has passed from death to life.

John 5:24

For God so loved the world, that he gave his only Son, that whoever believes in him should not perish but have eternal life. For God did not send his Son into the world to condemn the world, but in order that the world might be saved through him.

John 3:16-17

For by grace you have been saved through faith. And this is not your own doing; it is the gift of God, not a result of works, so that no one may boast.

Ephesians 2:8-9

If you confess with your mouth that Jesus is Lord and believe in your heart that God raised him from the dead, you will be saved. For with the heart one believes and is justified, and with the mouth one confesses and is saved.

Romans 10:9-10

Because our sin has separated us from God, we need a Savior, one who would take our place in eternal death and give us eternal life. Jesus is that Savior; the only one qualified to take our place.

And this is the testimony, that God gave us eternal life, and this life is in his Son. Whoever has the Son has life; whoever does not have the Son of God does not have life.

1 John 5:11-12

Receive Christ right now by praying a prayer such as this one. Speak the words from your heart, and God will hear and answer you.

> *Dear God, I see that my sins have separated me from You, and I repent of sin. Thank You that you loved me so much that You sent Jesus to suffer and die on my behalf, so that I could receive eternal life. I believe Jesus died for me and rose again, and I receive Him as my Savior right now. Jesus, You are my Lord, and I'll live for You from this day on. Thank You, Father, for saving me!*

If you prayed that prayer and meant it, be assured that God has done exactly what you asked. You are now His child. You have been born into His family. This verse now describes you, the new creation:

> *Therefore, if anyone is in Christ, he is a new creation. The old has passed away; behold, the new has come.*
>
> *2 Corinthians 5:17*

There are some additional steps you should take now that you are a follower of Jesus Christ. The most important step is to find a good local church. The pastor there will minister to you and help you grow in the things of God. Make sure your church believes and teaches the Bible and allows the Holy Spirit to work freely. Your pastor can help teach you about other steps to get started in the Christian life, such as studying the Word of God, being filled with the Holy Spirit, tithing, and serving in the local church.

Congratulations on making life's most important decision!

About the Author

Faith in God's Word, and constant reliance on the Holy Spirit have been the keys to success in the life and ministry of Rev. Joel Siegel. Raised and educated as a Jew, Joel Siegel, at age 18, had a life-transforming encounter with Christ that brought him true purpose and fulfillment.

Rev. Siegel began preaching and teaching the Word of God soon after he was saved in 1986. He entered full-time ministry in 1990, serving for three years as the music director for the gospel music group *Truth*. Truth's road schedule took Joel and his wife Amy worldwide to over 300 cities a year, ministering in churches and on college campuses.

From 1993 to 2000, Joel was the musical director for Rev. Kenneth E. Hagin's RHEMA Singers & Band. In addition to assisting Rev. Hagin in his crusade meetings, Joel produced eight music projects for the ministry, including his first solo release, *Trust & Obey*.

From 2000 to 2011, Joel and Amy (herself a skilled pastor and worship leader), served as the founding pastors of Good News Family Church in Orchard Park, NY. During this time, they were frequently asked to host shows for the TCT Christian Television Network. Joel regularly hosted their popular *Ask The Pastor* program.

Rev. Siegel spends his time ministering to congregations in the U.S. and abroad, passionately endeavoring to fulfill his assignment to help lead this generation into the move of God that will usher in the return of Christ.

The Siegels make their home in Colorado. Joel oversees Faith Church Colorado in the town of Castle Rock, where Amy is lead pastor.

For music recordings, audio teaching series, books, and other resources, or to invite Rev. Joel to minister at a church or event, please visit www.joelsiegel.org.